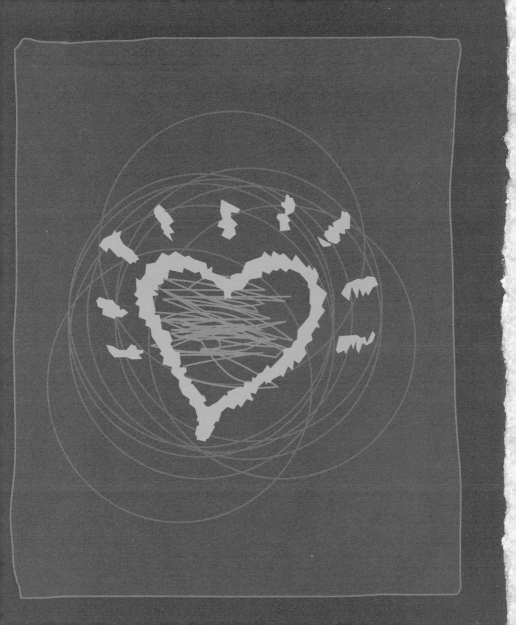

love
notes

Also by Jim Brickman

Simple Things—a book written with Cindy Pearlman

Greatest Hits—a collection of some of Jim's biggest
hit love songs and romantic instrumentals

Visit **www.JimBrickman.com** for exclusive offers on
music, DVDs, clothing, Jim's V.I.P. Club, and more

Hay House Titles of Related Interest

Little Things Make a Big Difference, by Laurin Sydney

Pleasant Dreams, by Amy E. Dean

A Relationship for a Lifetime, by Kelly E. Johnson, M.D.

Secrets of Attraction, by Sandra Anne Taylor

All of the above are available at your local bookstore,
or may be ordered by visiting:
Hay House USA: **www.hayhouse.com**
Hay House Australia: **www.hayhouse.com.au**
Hay House UK: **www.hayhouse.co.uk**
Hay House South Africa: **orders@psdprom.co.za**

love notes

101 Lessons from the Heart

Jim Brickman and Cindy Pearlman

HAY HOUSE, INC.
Carlsbad, California
London · Sydney · Johannesburg
Vancouver · Hong Kong

Published and distributed in the United States by: Hay House, Inc., P.O. Box 5100, Carlsbad, CA 92018-5100 · *Phone:* (760) 431-7695 or (800) 654-5126 · *Fax:* (760) 431-6948 or (800) 650-5115 · www.hayhouse.com · **Published and distributed in Australia by:** Hay House Australia Pty. Ltd., 18/36 Ralph St., Alexandria NSW 2015 · *Phone:* 612-9669-4299 · *Fax:* 612-9669-4144 · www.hayhouse.com.au · **Published and distributed in the United Kingdom by:** Hay House UK, Ltd. · Unit 62, Canalot Studios · 222 Kensal Rd., London W10 5BN · *Phone:* 44-20-8962-1230 · *Fax:* 44-20-8962-1239 · www.hayhouse.co.uk · **Published and distributed in the Republic of South Africa by:** Hay House SA (Pty), Ltd., P.O. Box 990, Witkoppen 2068 · *Phone/Fax:* 2711-7012233 · orders@psdprom.co.za · **Distributed in Canada by:** Raincoast · 9050 Shaughnessy St., Vancouver, B.C. V6P 6E5 · *Phone:* (604) 323-7100 · *Fax:* (604) 323-2600

Editorial supervision: Jill Kramer   *Design:* Amy Rose Szalkiewicz

Library of Congress Cataloging-in-Publication Data

Brickman, Jim.
    Love notes : 101 lessons from the heart / Jim Brickman and Cindy Pearlman.
        p. cm.
    ISBN 1-4019-0608-7 (hardcover)
    1. Love. I. Pearlman, Cindy, 1964-. II. Title.
    BF575.L8B724 2004
    152.4'1--dc22

                              2004020842

                          ISBN: 1-4019-0608-7

              08 07 06 05   4 3 2 1
                  1st printing, January 2005

              Printed in the United States of America

This book is dedicated to
Sally Brickman and Paul Pearlman:
Thank you from the bottom
of our hearts for teaching us about love.

"Like the stars over dark fields, love is the gift of eternal forces. We do not know why it appears; it is just the song the universe sings to itself."

— Zen master John Tarrant

Contents

PART II : LESSONS ON UNCONDITIONAL LOVE

PART III: LESSONS ON ROMANTIC LOVE

PART IV: LESSONS ON MAKING IT WORK

PART V: LESSONS ON REAL LOVE

(**Note**: These stories are inspired by real-life events, but the names and various identifying details of certain individuals have been changed to protect privacy.)

All celebrity stories are reprinted
with permission of Big Picture News Inc.
All song lyrics are reprinted by permission of Jim Brickman.

Introduction

This Is a True Story

A human being has a one in 600,000 chance of being hit by lightning. The odds are against it, but that means absolutely nothing if you're the person who's struck. This book is filled with true stories about people who got hit by something just as intense and as rare as lightning. It's called love.

That's what happened to Jessica and Sam. So please suspend disbelief, because what you're about to read actually happened—the words are exact, and nothing has been embellished for the purposes of making up an even better yarn. People forget that truth is often stranger than fiction and that real stories can be richer than fantasy. But that's jumping ahead. For now, just trust completely in love for a couple minutes (or a bit longer if you're either skeptical or a slow reader).

Come on along for the ride.

Flight of Fancy

They met at dusk, which is probably the only time something beautiful could happen at an airport. All it took was a man, a woman, and space—the scary part was bridging the gap. In this case, it was a distance of about 20 feet, and she refused to perform the old shy, glance-past-each-other dance. Instead, she looked directly at him, and what followed could only be described as magic.

She was the bolder of the two, which explains why a rational woman 33 years of age would invade a total stranger's personal space. (Of course, the 38-year-old man's broad shoulders; dark, curly hair; and warm eyes were also greatly to blame.) Maybe his eyes gave her silent permission to keep walking toward him until just inches separated their faces. That's when she took a deep breath and gave him a hug.

"Hello, I'm home," Jessica announced with all the bravado she could muster. Inside, she was thinking, *This is absolutely insane, but it's the only thing I can say to this man because he looks like home to me.* Win or lose, she had to say those exact words because they were true—and sometimes the truth is all you have.

Life is a series of tiny moments. Sam could have jolted back in shock, walked past Jessica, or even called for airport security. But he didn't. Instead, he felt an immediate connection. "It's good to have you home," he said, not skipping a beat. He didn't quite know where those words came from—he simply knew that he had to say them because his entire being felt them.

What started as an unlikely greeting between strangers in a strange land moved on to the stages of modern courtship, including e-mails and late-night phone calls that lasted until dawn. It wasn't long before Sam and Jessica knew that life would be unbearable unless they could be together. So she packed her bags and moved from Boston to Chicago to live with the soul mate she'd searched for all her life. People who met them, even the ones who didn't believe in love at first sight, couldn't deny it: These two were living the dream.

Did this couple's instantaneous attraction last? Well, Sam and Jessica married and . . . you'll have to read the rest of their story later in this book. Need a hint? Let's just say that The Beatles had it wrong when they sang, "All you need is love." Sometimes you need a little bit more. . . .

About Love Notes

Jessica and Sam's love story serves as an opening to this book because it demonstrates that love comes from a place where even the most bitter and cynical of us dwell: the heart.

This book has a simple purpose—to reveal true stories of everyday people (and several famous ones) who have lived lives full of courage, adventure, challenge, and bravery. These stories are here to enlighten, inspire, and educate, but they'll also make you laugh and maybe even shed a few tears. Of course, real life doesn't always have storybook endings. Love is tested every single day, but the good news is that it survives.

The idea for *Love Notes* began a few years ago during a phone conversation between pop composer Jim Brickman and his friend, entertainment reporter and author Cindy Pearlman. Jim was working on an album of love songs, while Cindy was complaining about seeing one too many Hollywood movies about love. "These movies really stink," she moaned. "I bet you could go next door to my neighbors' house and hear a better story about real-life love."

Jim agreed, noting, "My fans tell me these stories all the time. It's amazing what average people go through in their lives, and these stories inform my music."

And that's what inspired this book, which began with simply asking people for their stories and then posting a notice on Jim's Website for interested fans to share their most personal recollections. What began as two or three letters a day became hundreds of messages per week over a year's time. The rest is history—told on the slips of paper and coffee-stained notes that poured in, or in e-mails that were sent two or three times by very eager romantics who wanted to make sure they arrived.

People spun their stories over dinners that got cold or while children were playing in the background. And the couples who told them took turns playfully arguing about the details:

"Honey, I was wearing a pink dress when we met."
"No, it was the red one with the lace."
"Oh, you're right. But you were in that blue suit."
"I've never owned a blue suit."

We also gathered some stories from a few famous folks because most celebrities insist that what they desire most of all isn't money or fame, it's love. (Okay, some stars *do* want to cuddle up at night with their bank statements and press clippings, but they're not in this book!)

It would be disingenuous to say that the people whose stories appear in this book simply kissed and told. Instead, they began to reveal themselves little by little. So why did they choose to volunteer their stories? Maybe because happiness expands when it's shared, or perhaps because it helps to know that others have come out of personal suffering with open hearts.

These stories suggest that there's no such thing as perfect love, and that even the most seemingly divine and blessed relationships have their crisis points. What the people in *Love Notes* illustrate is that through courage, hard emotional work, and a belief in the power of love, they didn't lose faith in each other.

The way Jim sees it, when he sits down to compose a love song, he's filled "with pure idealism. I want to believe with every fiber in my being that it's possible to give your heart and soul to someone, whether it be a mate, a child, a parent, a pet, or the world."

While romantic bliss with a soul mate is almost everyone's ideal, we need to remember that there are other types of love out there that are just as good. That's why this book is broken down into different categories and includes stories that reflect love for a child, love for a parent, romantic love, love in a time of turmoil, unconditional love, love of a pet, and altruistic love, among other chapters. And while there are many useful tips in each slice-of-life saga, we've topped each vignette with a few pointers called "Love Lessons" that seemed the most poignant to us and needed to get the spotlight. A few stories have more lessons because they took so many twists and turns, but feel free to let your own heart seek out what it wants to learn from those who have lived these tales.

It comes down to one simple thing: It's not about who gets your heart, it's about the giving of it. Is there anything better or more pure that we can offer another human being? As Jim shares, "I've observed a lot of love each night when I'm in concert, and, afterward, I've spent many hours talking to the fans about it. Specifically, I want to know what they've figured out during their time on the planet because I certainly don't have all the answers. To sum it up, I'm told that those happiest in love do adopt a certain 'ignorance is bliss' motto. In other words, they don't walk around intellectualizing and dissecting this love thing too much." He adds, "The bottom line is, if you think too much about love, you don't leave yourself open to feeling it."

In the end, the message of *Love Notes* is simple and forthright: Basically, all you can be is hopeful in love. Hopeful for a soul mate. Hopeful that your child gives you a kiss on the cheek when he runs in after school. Hopeful that your mom and dad know how much they really mean to you. Hopeful that the world can take a minute and find a little love, too. It's not too much to ask. (Oh, and if you have any ideas on this subject, please feel free to drop us a note at **www.jimbrickman.com**.)

Part I

Lessons on Family

"When I was a little girl, my father took me to Paris. Later, I asked him why. He said, 'For the rest of your life, you'll always know that the first time you went to Paris, it was with a man who truly loved you and will love you for the rest of your life.'"

— Gwyneth Paltrow on her father,
the late Bruce Paltrow

LOVE LESSONS

1. Love overrides all types of tragedy.

2. Reliability and family loyalty are very special kinds of love.

3. For better or worse, a parent's love is often the most pure.

Chapter 1
A Wedding in Flames

The sooty, smudged note read, "Honey, I'll be back soon. We had a small fire, but don't worry. Love, Dad."

With mounting dread, I began to think, *Oh God, not today. This is my wedding day! The air is supposed to be filled with the smell of roses and the sweet scent of hope and joy, not ashes and ruin.*

Hands shaking, I grabbed my car keys. I knew that it wasn't my parents' home that was on fire because I was standing in their sunny yellow kitchen. It seemed only right to spend my last night as a single woman in the house where I grew up. Mom made her famous mac and cheese, and I'd had a wonderful night with my parents talking about life, love, and how they'd created the most amazing marriage.

When I'd gone to bed, the dreams that filled my head must have prevented me from hearing the phone ring at four in the morning. In my unconscious bliss, I hadn't heard the fire department calling to say that our family business was going up in flames. As I slept, I was spared the fact that I was losing a sibling—no, not one of the flesh-and-blood variety, but one just as precious to my parents as my sister and me. I know it sounds strange, but this business was treated like another child in our family.

My heart sank as I remembered how it took my parents 15 years to build a textile store based on a craft that had been in our family for more than 100 years. It was called Oak Brothers, and the business was built on sweat and sacrifice. Established in 1886, our family had originally made the fabric for covered wagons. Over the years, the modern version of a beautiful fabric business had become something so special because our entire family worked there, and now that life and the closeness it created was in peril.

Holding my breath, I dialed the business's number. A recording came on to say, "We're sorry, but this line is no longer in service."

Before I could drop the receiver, call-waiting clicked on, and when I answered, my mother's friend Bev immediately said, "Oh, hon, I'm so sorry."

"W-what are you talking about?" I stammered.

"Uh . . . I better not tell you," she said nervously. She didn't want to be the one to break the bad news on my wedding day.

"Tell me. *Tell me right now!*" I demanded.

"Honey, everything is gone," she said. "It's a total loss."

Looking at the fresh flowers on the kitchen table and then at my bridal veil hanging near the staircase, I could hardly breathe. What do you do when part of your world comes crashing down? Before I could even think one thought about what to do, the kitchen door opened and my mother walked in with tears streaming down her face. "Your father wants to see you," she said, looking like a woman who had lost something irreplaceable.

The business was only a few miles from my parents' home, but it seemed as if we drove for days in silence to get there. As our old family station wagon rounded the corner, I saw fire trucks lining a street bathed in ashes, which were floating through the air like giant gray snowflakes. A black, charred silhouette barely resembling a building was all that was left of Oak Brothers.

"Honey, it was a bad wire—it sparked and ignited some chemicals," said my dad, who stood in the street with red, swollen eyes. I knew that I'd never forget that defeated look on the face of a man who embodied the saying "Like a rock."

My parents huddled close to me as our fragile constitutions crumbled. I was in shock, and my mother was shaking so hard from her sobs that she could barely speak. My father couldn't keep the little bit of bravado he had left. One tiny tear formed, and I saw it slowly slip across his cheek.

As the ashes from the building swirled around us and attached themselves to our tears, I knew that there was only one thing that I could do under the circumstances. "Daddy, we're not going to hold the wedding. We'll do it another time," I said, meaning it. How could I possibly celebrate on this day of all days?

My father took my face into his big hands, looked at me with great resolve, and said, "Now this is your day—we'll take care of the rest of this stuff later. We've got a wedding to go to. There are very few problems in this life that can't wait until Monday morning."

That day, we went to my wedding with smiles on our faces that weren't masking pain. Our hearts were open and genuine because we knew that a building didn't matter—the foundation of our family could never be destroyed. It's unbelievable, but most of our out-of-town guests never even knew what was really behind our early-wedding-day tears.

Yes, fire can destroy, but a strong love can only build. I discovered that foundation of life in my new husband, but I also saw the entire structure in the faces of my parents, whose love stood firm against the ruins.

Epilogue: At the time of the fire, there was a man who owed my father $13,000 for textiles but was facing bankruptcy. Instead of payment, he gave my father the use of his building for business purposes for as long as my father needed. The phone company restored the Oak Brothers number by Tuesday morning. My parents missed exactly one day of business. The fire had a lasting effect, however, and my parents recently sold the company. Now the only thing they have to worry about is where to go as they tour America in their new RV! (By the way, their problems still wait for Monday mornings.)

— **Inspired by Amy from Portland, Oregon**

Chapter 2

Stevie's Wish

The word *love* was ruined for me by the age of 32. If you want to put it in playground terms, my heart was screaming, "I give up!" It's not that any particular boyfriend had cheated on me or broken my heart—quite simply, I'd just never met anyone who was "it," and I was tired of waiting.

The movie of my life was a lonely story. "Maybe I've seen too many films and read too many romance novels," I sighed to a friend. "We form this idea of what love *should* be instead of what it actually is."

As I watched beautiful actors come together in dark cinemas and read about handsome cowboys living alone on ranches just waiting for special women to capture their hearts, I became a little sad. I soon came to the conclusion that this type of love truly didn't exist in real life, so I stopped dreaming of it.

Despite my newfound practicality about romance, I still had a lot of love to give, so I began teaching children with chronic and life-threatening illnesses at St. Christopher's Hospital for Children in New Jersey. And in 1997, my relationship with one of the loves of my life began. His name was Stevie, and the seven-year-old boy and I got to know each other very well. His spirit wasn't clouded by the fact that his body was failing and his little lungs were growing weaker from cystic fibrosis.

A child's heart has a funny way of triumphing over illness. Stevie actually got better and left the hospital, which was a joyous day for everyone. Soon after he went home, I got a call at work. "Hi, Erin, it's your friend Stevie," said the sweet voice on the other end of the phone. "I miss you, and I just wanted to say 'Hi.'" This was better than any movie, because instead of my heart skipping a beat, it was suddenly very full.

But little Stevie wasn't content to just pick up a telephone. Spotting me one day online, he wrote: "Hi, Erin! Now we can talk to each other all the time, and I won't have to miss you so much."

"Oh, that's just what I need!" I teased him. "Now I'll have Stevie popping up on my computer screen whenever I'm trying to get some work done!"

"It's your lucky day!" he teased right back.

My pint-sized friend came from a stereotypical Italian family who'd fill his hospital room with homemade lasagna and pizza that smelled so good you begged for a bite. (It's a good thing that Stevie insisted on sharing with anyone who popped their head into his room!) Wise beyond his years, Stevie told me one evening, "I know that the most important thing in life is loving your family. But, Erin, you don't really have one—you're not married, and I don't think you even have a boyfriend to be nice to you."

Rolling my eyes, I prodded him to eat his dinner, but Stevie wouldn't veer from the subject at hand, which was my lonely life. "Don't you want to get married?" he continued. "If you do, you can have kids, and then you can have grandkids. So then when you die there will be a lot of people at your funeral."

"Stevie, eat your food!" I ordered, dismissing his comments by making the "monster face" he loved so much. Yet deep down, I couldn't help but admit that the husband-and-kids-filled scenario Stevie wished for me sounded blissful. I always knew that the most important thing in life is the love of one's family.

As for Stevie's family, I got to know them pretty well, too. I heard all the Pantinni family secrets because nothing was off-limits for this young man. In no time, I heard about the clan's wild New Year's Eve parties, and I found out about the exciting life of Stevie's beloved Uncle Joe. "Uncle Joe is a policeman," Stevie informed me. "He's single and raising his four babies 'cause his wife cheated on him and left him with all those kids. She's a total bitch!"

"Stevie!" I scolded. "Don't use that kind of language."

"Well, what kind of woman leaves a guy with four kids?" Stevie demanded, and I had to admit that he had a point. "They had a really bad divorce," he continued.

"What do you know about bad divorces?" I asked the seven-year-old.

"Lots!" he replied. "My uncle's ex made up lots of lies about him and told them in a court of law."

Poor Uncle Joe, I thought. I also found myself thinking that he sounded like a great guy considering that he hadn't run away from raising those kids all alone.

One day, Stevie beamed at me with his irresistible smile. "Erin, I want you to marry my Uncle Joe!" he announced with gusto.

Laughing, I asked, "Why in the world do you want me to do that?"

Without pause, Stevie took the deepest breath possible for him and said clearly, "Because I love you and want you to be in my family." Stunned, I just stared at him and tried to blink back tears. "Oh, and my other reason is because you don't cook and he's Italian like me, so he can always cook good stuff for you," the boy added.

"Uh-huh," I nodded.

"Oh, and Uncle Joe has four kids," Stevie grinned.

"Uh-huh," I repeated. "You told me about his kids."

"Badda-boom, badda-bing, instant family!" Stevie concluded, raising his little fists in the air in a sign of victory. And he wouldn't stop heckling me—even as I tried to leave the room to look in on another patient. "Four kids, Erin. You won't have to get all fat and pregnant!" he yelled.

Before long, the idea of my marrying Uncle Joe had become a joke in the Pantinni family. Even *I* had to laugh because I was suddenly "engaged" mentally to someone I'd never even met.

Letting Go . . . and Believing Again

Meanwhile, months passed with the occasional instant message from Stevie . . . and then one morning I was jolted awake by the phone.

"Erin, I just want to prepare you," said Melanie, my co-worker at the hospital. "Stevie was admitted again, and he's not doing well. They're not even sure if he'll make it through the night."

That next week was the most difficult of my life. It was two weeks before Christmas, and I'd leave the hospital at night and walk into the bitter New Jersey air, not even feeling the chill. My mind was much too preoccupied with begging God to let Stevie go peacefully. Knowing that his death would deeply affect the hospital staff, I tried to keep my emotions buried and help my friends at work. Everyone loved Stevie so much that many of us offered to be tested to see if we could donate a lung to him, but that just wasn't possible.

On the morning of December 11, Stevie's father came to see me. "Erin, it's time to say good-bye," he said with tears shimmering in his eyes.

Knowing that this would be the darkest day of my fortunate life, I spent the next several hours at the child's bedside with his family. Even though he was barely conscious, we told Stevie the stories he found the funniest because, more than anything, he loved to laugh and make others do the same. So, chuckling and crying at the same time, we held his hand and thought about how much this little boy had brought to our lives during his short time on Earth.

Hours passed, and then Stevie's grandmother came to the door. Praying it wasn't bad news, I closed my eyes. What followed was a total shock. "Erin," she said, "I'd like to introduce you to someone. This is Joe—you know, the one Stevie wants you to marry."

It's hard to explain what I felt in those next seconds. All I can remember is that I wasn't able to move in the presence of this tall, wide-shouldered man who'd almost become folklore to me by now. Joe and I stared at each other for a few seconds before I looked away to regain my composure.

"Hi, Erin. I'm mortified by that introduction," Joe said softly, staring at me and then at his nephew, who looked so small and frail in that large hospital bed.

"Don't worry. They've been teasing me forever," I said. "By the way, it's nice to finally meet you, but these circumstances . . ."

"I know," Joe said, his voice breaking. In the next few minutes, it was clear that the man was overcome with emotion. Looking at an almost-lifeless Stevie, he stood very far away from the rest of his family and seemed intimidated by the hospital setting. Unlike the rest of the group, he didn't know the doctors and nurses who had gathered in great numbers outside the child's door.

Since I felt bad for him, I talked to Joe about his wonderful nephew. "I feel so guilty because I never came to see him when he was in here before," Joe told me. "It was just too hard to see him that sick."

"It doesn't matter. It never mattered to Stevie," I said, reassuringly. "He understood that his big Uncle Joe was out there chasing bad guys and taking care of his four kids. He loved you for being such a great guy. In fact, he talked about you all the time."

Joe's eyes welled up, and he seemed genuinely touched. "He called me and talked about you, too."

Knowing that we needed to lighten the mood, I tried a feeble attempt at a joke: "Besides, he had very high standards for me, and he chose you. He wouldn't want me to marry just anyone."

Gazing hard into my eyes, Joe gave me a hint of a smile and then left the room to gather his emotions.

At 4 P.M. that day, as the winter sun slipped away, so did our Stevie. He passed as his entire family gathered around his bed in prayer. Suddenly, I felt odd about joining them during such a personal moment. But Stevie's mother saw me standing alone in the hallway and said, "Come in here. You're family."

Afterward, I locked myself in my office and sobbed uncontrollably for what seemed like hours. Not knowing what to do or where to go, I began to wander around the hospital, because the idea of going home to my empty house made me want to scream. Nobody would understand how much I loved Stevie. No one knew how close we'd become over the last year. So, as I meandered through the cold, sterile hallways in a daze, I gave in to my grief until I bumped into a large, immovable object.

"Excuse me," I mumbled. Then I looked up. "Oh, it's you!"

"I need to get out of here," Joe said. "Do you want to go get a drink?"

"To Stevie," I said over a glass of wine.

"To Stevie," Joe repeated.

We spent the next seven hours talking, until the sun came up again and it was a brand-new day. All I can remember from that night, however, is breaking down in tears time and time again. Joe would take my hand in his and simply say, "Everything is going to be okay, I promise. And Stevie wouldn't want to see you this sad."

We talked about our lives and what we wanted for ourselves. It was strange, but this "familiar stranger" and I seemed to agree on everything. Most important, our ideas of marriage and raising children were identical.

When Joe told me funny stories about his past and his family, I couldn't help but smile. "Why do I get the feeling that you already know all this?" he asked, smiling back at me.

"There are no secrets in your family," I reminded him.

As dawn broke, he suddenly appeared to be a little bit nervous. Wondering if he was worried about his kids, I asked if he needed to go home—but his children weren't the cause of Joe's concern. "Erin, I'm wondering how inappropriate it would be to ask for your phone number," he confessed.

"It would be very inappropriate," I replied. "But I'd give it to you in a second."

Our romance began in this very nontraditional way, although Joe was a traditional man. A delivery arrived at my workplace the following day: a bouquet of 11 red roses surrounding 1 white rose for Stevie. The card read: "Thank you for making a difference. Joseph." A few days later, I received more roses, but this time there were two white ones surrounded by ten red blooms. On the card, he'd written a quote straight from *Romeo and Juliet*. Then later that night, as I wandered in from work late, the phone rang.

"Hi, it's Joe," said the distinctly male voice on the other end of the line. "I just want to make sure you're okay." Four hours later when I hung up, I realized that I'd never even taken off my coat.

It only seemed natural for Joe and me to help each other get through the tough weeks ahead. I'm not sure how it happened, but during that time we began to spend our nights cuddled up on the couch in front of the fireplace, just talking, kissing, and listening to music. We even did something so silly, yet so meaningful, when we danced in our socks in the middle of my kitchen.

Two weeks after we met, he looked at me one night and said, "I love you, and I want to marry you someday." Two weeks after that, he got down on one knee and asked, "Will you be my wife?"

Six months after meeting, Joe and I were married, and I became the mother of his four beautiful children. It's funny that married life hasn't changed much for us, because we still spend our nights cuddled up in front of the fireplace listening to beautiful music. We talk about Stevie as much as possible and are convinced that he brought us together. It was almost as if God had to strip us down to our most vulnerable state in order for us to receive the gift He was about to give us. We thank Him every single day. And we thank Stevie, too.

— **Inspired by Erin from Newark, New Jersey**

LOVE LESSONS

6. Your partner's dream can also become your dream.

7. Even in the bleakest of times, sheer will combined with love wins every time.

Chapter 3

Tough-Guy Love, Part 1
(Featuring Bernie Mac)

He was one of the faceless: the anonymous man working on the fishing docks, the mover whom people ignored, and the UPS driver who didn't warrant a second glance. And when Bernie Mac was a janitor at the University of Illinois in Chicago, kids used to dump their trash at his feet, not caring that he only ate if he cleaned up their messes.

As with many working men, there was a moment when something just snapped. He figures that first big Mac attack happened in 1988: "I was a sales rep for Wonder bread, and I was miserable," says the Chicago native. "I was performing comedy for no money at night, getting home at two in the morning, and then getting up at four to deliver bread."

That Thanksgiving Day, Bernie had 2,000 loaves of bread on his truck and some half-baked ideas about stardom as a comedian. In weather so cold that his breath froze in midair, he pulled up to a grocery store and called the company. "I said, 'I'm sorry, but you have to pick up your truck. I'm quitting to become a comedian.'"

It's ironic, but he worried most about dough—specifically, how he was going to tell his beloved wife, Rhonda, who'd also been his high school sweetheart, that he was no longer going to be the family breadwinner.

At the time, Bernie and his wife were living poor. He recalls that in a 30-degree-below-zero winter, their heat was actually cut off. "We were surviving on those tiny space heaters that can kill you and catch your house on fire," he says.

Yet Bernie came home to that freezing-cold house and couldn't find the nerve to tell his wife that he'd just quit his job. But he didn't like to keep any secrets from her either, so on the way to a family dinner that night, he blurted out the news. He told her that he'd ditched the paycheck that was keeping them in such "luxury."

"If I can't be who I am, I will die. If I can't do comedy, this life is not worth living," he said, waiting for her to say that she was leaving him for a better life.

But for Rhonda, there *was* no better life without this man. That's why she looked at her beloved husband's tormented face, smiled, and said, "I'm really with you, guy."

"That is love—unconditional love," says Bernie, who is now, incidentally, a major movie and television star. "I could have never done it without Rhonda's support. Even when I made eight dollars a week as a stand-up in the beginning—and that check bounced— she believed. On the nights when we'd shiver under those covers, she'd say to me, 'Bernie, I'm still with you, guy.'"

LOVE LESSONS

8. Don't be afraid to melt for love.

9. Loyalty means everything.

Chapter 4

Pappi

This is a story about a very special love.

How many people do you know who get to choose their own father? Well, I did. Of course, I didn't know that I had such an option because as a child I lived with my mother and baby brother, John, in a small military town in Louisiana.

We didn't have a daddy, but we weren't alone: My grandparents lived two blocks away in a fine home with a little bungalow next door that they rented out as a way to "provide for the extras." Granny was our savior, babysitting while my single mother earned money for the important things to a little girl, such as new dolls and, even better, big chocolate ice-cream cones, which were my favorite thing in the entire world.

A precocious child (or so I've been told), I was known for wandering away, which didn't exactly please my mama or my granny. "Candy, don't you ever leave the house without a grown-up!" my mama constantly warned.

She was speaking to deaf ears, because as much as I wanted to mind her, I had a big, huge, wonderful world to discover. Even though I was only four years old, I can still remember the day I escaped my grandmother's house looking for an afternoon thrill. I wanted ice cream, and I was no fool. Every day I'd see Granny wander off to the bungalow next door because that's where there was a big square freezer. If Granny could find ice cream in that white metal box, then I certainly thought that *I* could toddle over there and sneak a cone before anyone noticed that I was missing.

Laughing, I snuck through the bungalow's open screen door and found the freezer. It was easy to open, but that ice cream was up high, so I climbed on a step stool. Minutes later, I had a face that was smeared in chocolate.

"Now who do we have here eating all the ice cream?" asked a deep male voice.

Oh no! It was the big man who lived in the bungalow! He'd startled me, so I ran right back into Granny's house. But the very next day, I didn't care about that big man. All I wanted in life was more ice cream, so I snuck next door again. This time it wasn't so easy, because the man was sitting at the kitchen table eating an egg-salad sandwich for lunch.

"Hi, Mister," I said, suddenly not afraid at all because he looked like a nice man with all that egg falling on his chin. Maybe we could be friends . . . but there was one thing first. "I want some ice cream," I announced. "But don't tell Granny!"

Smiling down at me, he replied, "I thought you might be back. What's your name? Where do you live?"

"I'm Candy, and my granny lives over in the next yard. My mommy is at work," I said.

If this interrogation lasted much longer, I probably would have given him our phone number and my mother's birthday. I know how it sounds in this day and age, but back then it was a simple time, and we didn't know any better. I was lucky that this was a very good man.

"Okay, Candy. I'm going to make you one scoop of ice cream, but you'd better eat it in your granny's yard so that she doesn't worry about you," the man said, reaching for a metal scooper.

Looking up at him, I noticed that he had a nice face with big green eyes and a few wrinkles.

"Now come with me," he said after handing me my treat. "I'm taking you and your ice-cream cone back to your grandmother." A few minutes later, I was back on Granny's porch, and she was thanking the man for bringing me home. Then to me, she asked, "Candy, what did I say about wandering?"

Watching my ice cream drip over my fingers, I promised to never go over there alone. I kept my word when the very next day I grabbed my little brother's hand and dragged him through the yard and over to the bungalow. John tried to knock on the back door and look sad in order to get his ice cream, but it didn't work. His knock was so faint that the man couldn't hear him. I finally yelled out, "Mister, do you got any ice cream? It's your friends from next door!"

Luckily, the nice man had *everything* in that freezer, including mint chocolate chip! This was better than plain chocolate, and my mother found me picking out the tiny chips and eating them separately on the man's back porch.

"Candy, I don't believe it!" Mama scolded, pretending to be mad. To the nice man, she said, "I'm so sorry they keep bothering you. They think you're the ice-cream man."

"It's really no trouble," he said. "My name is Jeff, ma'am. Would you like a scoop of mint chocolate chip?"

"I want one!" I said.

Jeff and my mother just laughed while he got out the scooper.

Over the next few months, Mama, John, and I visited Jeff all the time. He loved to have company, and I loved being in his kitchen. Jeff would let me go outside and pick wild onions for his spaghetti sauce. It made our mother grab her tummy when we teased her that we also put the mud from the onions into the sauce.

"That's what makes it extra yummy," Jeff said, winking at Mama. But he didn't just make funny faces at her—he also kissed her a few times, which made both John and me roll our eyes. (Secretly, we liked when he swung her around and gave her a hug.) They'd even leave us with Granny to go out dancing or to the movie house in town. Granny said that Mama and Jeff were falling in love, and she was right—soon they were married. I wondered if that made him our Pappi or just the ice-cream man who lived at our house.

One day I got my answer: "I love you and John so much that I want to adopt you. I want to be your daddy," Jeff said.

"Can I call you 'Pappi'?" I asked, because now that I was in school, I was one of the few kids without someone to call by that name.

"It would be the best day of my life if you did," he said, hugging me.

After the adoption papers were signed at the courthouse, we went out for—what else?—big scoops of ice cream. That tradition continued through birthdays and graduations or when boys at school were mean to me and Pappi wanted to cheer me up. I don't know where I'd be now without him. He's the one who picked me up when I fell, squashed big spiders that made me scream, and sent me off to my prom with tears in his eyes. He never held me back—instead, he let me wander through my life's adventures because the feeling to do so never ebbed in me. He taught me how to make homemade applesauce, and we swore to my mother that we left the mud from the apples in the sauce.

On my wedding day, Pappi walked me down the aisle with more than a few tears falling onto his new tux. Even as a grown-up, I talked to him almost every single day. I listened to his many fishing stories and never said a word when the fish got bigger, bigger, and even bigger. Jeff was my best friend, and then he became Grandpappi to my new baby daughter.

About ten months ago, Pappi was diagnosed with a rare cancer. Once I found out, I left my job to be with him in the hospital. Holding his hand after his radiation treatments, I reminded him how we met when I burglarized his house for his ice cream. He had to laugh, and the doctors just looked at him with shock. This certainly wasn't the time for laughter, but my Pappi was full of surprises. All I could do was hold his hand and tell him endlessly that I was the luckiest kid in the world. Who else could pick the very best father on Earth?

We were told eventually that the chemo was hurting Pappi's kidneys to the point that he couldn't have that treatment anymore. Radiation did very little, too. One day, the doctors came into his hospital room and told him that he had three to six months to live.

During that time, I spent every moment I could with Pappi talking about old times, looking at pictures, and remembering. Three months later, I lost the father I'd handpicked for myself all those years ago. I told my daughter that the angels came for him. Through these hard times, I try to remember to be thankful. I had a dad in my life who loved me unconditionally. I'll never forget how I adopted him in that little bungalow all those years ago.

I love you, Pappi.

— Inspired by Candy from New Orleans, Louisiana

LOVE LESSONS

10. Show no fear.

11. There's no such thing as a price tag on love, but jewelry is another matter.

Chapter 5

Tough-Guy Love, Part II
(Featuring Arnold Schwarzenegger)

Arnold Schwarzenegger's greatest loves are his four children, but that doesn't mean he's a "girlie man" as a parent. "They know when I mean business," says the governor of California, who adds, "My children can read my body language. I have a certain look and a certain voice."

He says that he parents with firm love: "My style of parenting is that I count to three. By three, things happen. This means that by two, my kids make sure they've straightened out their acts. If I'm counting in German, they know I *really* mean business," he says with a hearty laugh.

He quickly adds that "they're good kids and usually don't do anything wrong." In fact, those kids often do things that put huge grins on the faces of Arnold and his lovely wife, Maria Shriver. For example, "We went on a family vacation to Cabo San Lucas and my son negotiated the price of a necklace to buy me. He started out with $20, haggling with this guy on the beach. Later he came over and put it on my neck. With great pride my son said, 'I got it for $5, Daddy! Are you proud of me?'"

Oh, he was very proud indeed.

© Big Picture News Inc.

Chapter 6

Don't Walk Away

I'd been divorced for five years, but I wasn't bemoaning my singleness. That was a job for my closest confidante, Inez, who was relentless in telling me, "You've just got to get back out there."

As a single mom, I didn't have a road map to "out there," but I *could* navigate quite nicely to my living-room couch to watch movies on Lifetime. Apparently, this wouldn't do, so Inez practically kidnaped my remote control one day, informing me, "You have plans for Friday night."

"I have *what?*"

"I've set you up with a wonderful man named Timothy," my best buddy said in a breezy manner. I knew that she was waiting for me to put the kibosh on the whole thing, yet she was also hoping that I might just take a chance. But, as Inez knew, chances didn't come easily for me: I'd tried a few blind dates after the divorce, only to come home with stories about horny losers or men who needed a decade-long retreat with Dr. Phil because they had so many problems. Now there was another faceless man on deck. I wasn't interested.

"Really? How do you know that this Timothy is so wonderful?" I retorted, looking for reasons to pull the plug on this evening out because it wasn't even worth finding my eyeliner for. I didn't have the strength to think about outfits, let alone the mind-numbing small talk. *Nice summer we're having. How about those Bears? Oh right, they're the football team, not the baseball guys. Anyway, tell me about your childhood: Did you hate your mother? Did you cheat on your wife? If you're so amazing, then why are you single and looking?* That last one was the real question.

Inez interrupted this flow of negativity in my brain by saying, "Timothy is an amazing man. I mean, you can't argue with a guy who donated a kidney to his brother six months ago. Someone who donates a major organ deserves some company over a hamburger, dontcha think?"

I just hated it when Inez was right. Nevertheless, that Friday afternoon, I tried to push the date out of my mind as I slogged through a typical day at the bank where I worked as an accountant. Later that night, I put on a simple pair of beige slacks and a white sweater and waited for the "humanitarian of the year" to show up.

"Stop being so awful," I chastised myself. Just then a black SUV pulled up my driveway, and a man fumbled as he almost fell out of it. I smiled as I watched him continue this awkward dance, which included reaching back inside the vehicle to grab what looked like a bouquet of purple wildflowers.

Oh, I'm a terrible person. Just awful, I decided.

And when I opened the front door and looked into Timothy's nervous blue eyes, I didn't feel scared anymore. Instead, I thanked him for the flowers, smiling shyly as I left this tall drink of water with a mess of blond curls on my front porch. I had to step inside to find a vase, and I couldn't ask him in for reasons that had nothing to do with his being a stranger or that the house was a mess.

We weren't strangers for long, though. At dinner, I quickly decided that I liked Timothy's warm, gentle manners and the fact that he thought that what he'd done for his brother "wasn't such a big deal," although it was a very big sacrifice due to the complications that could have been involved. "It's family—you do what you have to do," he said, ketchup dripping down his chin.

I was tempted to wipe it away, but caught myself and handed him a napkin instead. Rolling his eyes and wiping his chin, Timothy looked more out of sorts than I felt. In a word, he was adorable.

Over the next couple of hours, I found out that the two of us had quite a lot in common, including a love of jazz music, antique shopping, and flea markets. Yet each time I discovered another sign that pointed to our compatibility, my heart sank a little bit further.

Even though I really liked Timothy, I knew that it was impossible to give in to that feeling. Our relationship could never start because it probably wouldn't finish happily. I'd been keeping something very important from him, and I worried that once he found out about it, he'd take the easy way out by running away. And I just didn't think I could face another rejection.

After fretting about this for several days, I decided to accept a second date with Timothy, who was so persistent that he stopped by the bank one morning with two cups of fancy coffee and more of those purple flowers that came from a field near his house. He suggested picking me up later that day for a sunset walk.

All day long, I was miserable. It just figured that I had a romantic date in my immediate future with a man I really liked but couldn't claim. After an uneasy afternoon, I finally resolved to tell Timothy the truth. I'd give him that reason to run, even though the thought of never seeing him again made me sad in such a profound way that I had to take a deep breath.

That evening as the orange summer sun began to set, I looked into Timothy's eyes but turned my head to avoid his kiss. I almost couldn't stand it if our first kiss was also our last. However, he needed to know the truth.

"Before we go any further, I think you need to know that my family life is a bit complicated," I began. It was a speech I'd recited many times in the past, and it *always* elicited the same response: "You're a very nice lady, but I don't need that kind of baggage."

I cleared my throat and continued. "My son, Justin, is physically disabled and in a wheelchair—he's also the most important part of my life. He's a wonderful boy with the heart of an angel, and he's sweet, funny, and loves to bust me because I don't know anything about sports. I don't know a goalie from a first baseman. And they both play football, right?" I tried a stab at humor. "Anyway, he's just about the most amazing kid in the whole world, but I'll understand if you don't want those complications in your own life," I concluded, my words flowing over each other in a mad, jumbled rush.

Good-bye, Timothy, I thought. *It would have been nice.*

I knew that the "Let's just be friends" song and dance that was certainly coming meant I wouldn't get another date with

Timothy. And had this been anyone but him, I wouldn't have cared so much.

Shaking myself out of my sadness, I concluded that I was a practical woman, and to that end I looked at the ground and waited for Timothy to pull away from me—after all, my life was pretty much a deal breaker. Yet he softly replied, "Why wouldn't I want to be more than friends with a woman who speaks so kindly and lovingly of her son?" Then he took one finger, placed it under my chin, tilted my head toward him . . . and kissed me.

A half hour later, we were pulling into my driveway when I saw my nine-year-old son sitting in the window. Knowing that his hawklike eyes were on the lookout for me, I smiled at how hard he was trying to be the man of the house. I stepped out of the SUV and motioned for him to join us outside.

Justin didn't need to be asked twice. He wheeled himself onto the front porch and said, "Hey, Mom, since you guys are so close to the car, could you go get us some ice cream?" he begged, holding his hands together like a prayer before adding, "Pretty please?"

"It's a few blocks away," I told Timothy, who was smiling warmly at Justin. At that moment, I knew that the next several minutes shouldn't be about me at all, but about my son getting to know my new friend.

"Hey, Justin, lead the way. I don't know this neighborhood, but I do know that I like chocolate," Timothy informed him. He added, "I also like the Cubs' chances this season."

"You like baseball?" Justin asked, his eyes dancing. "Know anything about getting some tickets?"

"Tickets to a Cubs game—is that football?" I teased. I knew the real answer, but liked the shocked look on both their faces.

"Girls," my new friend said, rolling his eyes at Justin, but then winking at me.

A year later, Timothy and I became engaged. Justin is planning to give his mother away to a man who deserves us both.

— Inspired by Janice from Hoffman Estates, Illinois.

LOVE LESSONS

13. You don't have to surrender, but when it comes to petty daily annoyances, just get over it.

14. Buy lots of paper towels for life's little messes.

Chapter 7

Meryl's Choice
(Featuring Meryl Streep)

Just in case you ever want to throw in the towel on marriage, think of Meryl Streep, arguably America's greatest living actress, who has been married to sculptor Donald Gummer for 23 years. "He's the glue of my life," Meryl says. "He's a great man, and we agree on the most important things. We disagree on almost all the little things, which really is no problem."

One major issue that they always agree to disagree on concerns a trait that her husband can't break: Donald scribbles on paper towels, and it aggravates every molecule of Meryl's celebrated being. "He can't keep track of phone numbers because he writes them down on pieces of paper towels," she explains. "Then he comes into the kitchen and says, 'Meryl, did you throw that out? I can't find that number anywhere.' And then he doesn't call people back because I used that paper towel to wipe up spilled orange juice on the counter. Silly me!"

In the interest of fairness, Meryl mentions that she isn't always a day at the beach. Ask her what her husband might list as her annoying habits, and she doesn't even need to breathe before answering. (She does cackle loudly, however.) "I can hear him say, 'She has an overbearing attention to detail!'" she cries. "If we're on a road trip, I'm plotting it out for weeks. It's annoying to him. And beyond that, I can't talk about him or he'll be appalled."

Chapter 8

A Boy Named Lad

My love story is about an incredible dog who lived his life in the midst of my ordinary family. He always seemed to know when I was happy or sad or when I needed him to be at my side. He *knew* my heart, and, later on, he *saved* my heart in a very special way.

Lad was a Shetland sheepdog who came to me when I was in the fourth grade. From the start he wasn't just a regular dog, but a member of our family who filled a unique role. Even as a puppy, he was intuitive: He'd sit outside, leaning against a tree, waiting for me to come home from school.

It was strange how Laddie knew when I was sad or tired—and he'd respond in the same manner so that I wouldn't feel so alone. If I was feeling joyous, he'd leap around the yard, sliding in the early-morning dew; but if I was sad, he'd just sit quietly next to me as I worked through my pain. He made himself available for petting, and allowed me to hold him even in that uncomfortably tight way that young children tend to grab dogs. Lad didn't flinch when I wept into his fur and treated him as if he were the warmest, most loving, furriest tissue on the planet. He could also sense when I'd calm down, and that would signal a different role for him. When the crisis was over, he'd bring a ball for me to throw to him, but he wouldn't play before doing his most important job: licking away my tears.

Laddie just always *knew*. And by the time I reached high school, he was my best friend and most trusted confidant in the world when I needed one most. At the time, I was being sexually abused and believed that I had nowhere to safely turn. Lad understood and stayed steady in his devotion and affection. He knew all my secrets, and when I felt like I was nothing, he continued to love and accept me just as I was. I can't even count how many tears Lad dried during those years. Our time together was the only happiness I experienced during my adolescence—he was a safe haven, and he helped me remember that love isn't unattainable.

He loved with complete devotion. How could life not be worth living with a love like that?

Eventually I went away to college and couldn't take Lad with me, which broke my heart. One day my parents phoned and told me that Lad wasn't eating. They knew that I could always get him to eat and wondered if there was a secret. The only secret we had was mutual trust. As the days passed, I could barely eat or sleep worrying about my beloved Laddie. And then the worst happened: Lad passed away in his sleep.

Feeling overwhelming grief in the depths of my heart, I almost collapsed when I heard the news. My best friend had died, and the only consolation was that he was no longer in any pain. Friends told me, "It's not like a person died. He was just a dog."

Just a dog. He was a loved one, a trusted companion, a life coach, my heart, and my soul. Sure, most pets are family members, but Lad wasn't merely a pet. He was the being I was closest to on this planet.

Years have passed, but I know that I'll always love my dear Laddie. I firmly believe that I'll see him again somewhere, someday, somehow. An incredible animal must have a soul—I don't question this idea, but know it as fact. Lad's capacity for love still outshines that of most people who are in my life now. Quite possibly, his was the greatest love I've ever known.

— Inspired by Megan from Phoenix, Arizona

LOVE LESSONS

16. Make the connection, and then feel lucky about it forevermore.

17. Value your partner above all else.

Chapter 9

Keeping the Faith
(Featuring Tim McGraw)

You've got to have Faith. And country singer Tim McGraw does—Faith Hill is his wife. Eight years of marriage and three children certainly spell happiness by Hollywood's or Nashville's standards.

They met on tour, and Tim recalls thinking, *Are you kidding? She's such a dog. . . .* But seriously, he says that he knew Faith was The One from the start: "How do you know? I think you know when you can't imagine it being any other way. Not being with this woman is not a thought I'll let enter my head."

And now he says that true love remains because "there isn't a day when I wake up and don't think, *The woman next to you is out of your league, buddy."* And, unlike many celebrity marriages, he says that the key is that it isn't about his star rising or hers soaring higher. He figures that there's plenty of room for two nice crooner homebodies to both hit it big. "There's no competition with us. Everything is good for us. It all goes to the same place, and we boost each other up," he says.

Chapter 10

Love Is a Roller-Coaster Ride

Ted and I were like any other couple planning a wedding: We were committed to each other, deeply in love, and losing our minds. I couldn't believe that our big day wasn't just going to be about our shared joy, but more about seating charts, napkins, and relatives who refused to be around each other. Welcome to the typical American nuptials.

One morning while I was trying to remember that this was the happiest time of my life (yeah, right), I heard the most ridiculous and wonderful offer over the car radio: "Hey, happy couples out there—are you engaged and bogged down by wedding plans? Well, we're going to marry a lucky twosome at your favorite amusement park. Just write us a letter and say why you should be that happy couple!" the smooth-talking DJ announced.

I raced home and got out a pad and a pen. "I'm losing the meaning of why I'm getting married," I wrote. "I need to get back on track." Two weeks later, Ted and I were married on a sunny morning at the amusement park. Vowing to love, honor, and respect each other forever, we said "I do" and then jumped into a hard plastic bucket seat for two. We fastened the safety harness around the new "us" and took a deep breath. As we took a ride together on that roller coaster, we didn't know that it wouldn't be our last.

You see, what Ted and I didn't know then is that the ride was symbolic: Our *lives* would turn out to be a roller-coaster ride, too. Now for three years we were on the "kiddie ride" where everything was rather smooth and uneventful. We did regular couple things together, including buying a home, decorating it, and talking about having children. Of course, "overjoyed" is the only way to describe the day we found out that I was pregnant, and 20 weeks later, one very nervous couple entered a doctor's office for their first sonogram.

The technician had seen scared faces like ours before and tried to put us at ease. "Oh, there's the leg!" he exclaimed. "Look at the abdomen! Two beautiful arms! And . . . oh." When the technician got to our child's heart, he abruptly stopped and said, "The doctor will be in soon."

There isn't a parent out there whose own heart wouldn't stop when a sonogram technician goes mute. Something was definitely wrong, and I suddenly felt very cold. Moments later, our worst fears were realized. "There's a problem with your baby's brain," the doctor said with great sorrow in his voice. Clutching Ted's hand, I began to sob softly.

"It's called Dandy-Walker Syndrome," the doctor went on to explain. "Your baby has a cyst in the fourth region of his brain. I just want you to know that it's not genetic, so it's not your fault. In fact, there's no reason for this to be happening."

We had no idea what Dandy-Walker was or what the long-term challenges were, but before we could even ask, the doctor made the idea of the long term seem like it wasn't even an option. "Your baby's chances of surviving this pregnancy and the birth are very slim," he explained, before adding even more heartbreaking news. "It probably won't survive—if it does, you're looking at serious heart problems, heart surgery, possible cleft palate, and developmental problems. You have an 80 percent chance of your child being severely retarded," he said.

In that one paragraph, a picture of our future had been painted: If our child even survived, his or her life would be about doctors, specialists, and therapists. Normalcy would be gone forever. "Most couples in this situation choose to terminate," the doctor added, glancing at the clock because his next appointment was waiting.

At that point, I looked at Ted. Once again, it was time to step on that roller coaster. "Doctor," Ted said calmly, "we don't need to continue this discussion. Terminating this pregnancy is not an option. This child is here. He's ours—no matter what happens, he is our child."

Then I spoke, and my words were clear and firm. "If our child doesn't survive this pregnancy, at least we have this time with him or her," I said. It wasn't a declaration said with great bravado or in a challenging way, it was soft and matter-of-fact. I was a mother who would take what time she could have with her child—no more and no less.

"It's up to you," the doctor sighed. "I just want to remind you that you're 20 weeks pregnant. You can only legally terminate up to 24 weeks in this state. I'd go home and give this some serious thought."

We did just that. We wept, held each other, and got on the Internet. Within days, we had assembled a team of specialists and genetic doctors who specialized in our baby's condition. A week later, our original sonogram doctor phoned. "I'm just calling to tell you that time is running out—but you still have options," he said. "I thought you might want to know that over 50 percent of cases with children who have Dandy-Walker are terminated in early pregnancy."

I hung up and vowed that the only option would be life for this child. To that end, I had sonograms each week to examine the problem cyst in our child's brain and monitor the development of its little heart. The specialists informed me that the baby would eventually need heart surgery, but that wasn't the worst of it. Each sonogram measured the growth of the baby's head, and it was growing abnormally large. "Please, God, don't let his head be any bigger," I prayed before each visit. Sometimes it *was* bigger, but sometimes it didn't change.

Week 27 gave us a new twist. Another sonogram technician was examining the baby and stopped suddenly. My heart sank. *Oh dear God, what now?* I thought, feeling that old dread again.

"Would you like to know if you're having a boy or a girl?" the smiling technician asked.

"I know we're having a girl. I just know it," Ted said, finding his sense of humor again. "It's my destiny to be outnumbered in my household."

I laughed joyously for the first time in weeks and shook my head. "I think it's a boy. I remember telling my mom about the baby being sick. I kept saying, 'I don't want him to die,'" I explained. "Even in her grief, Mom said, 'Wait, it's a him?' I told her I wasn't sure, but I am now." And I was right.

What else could we do but get ready for our son to enter the world? We painted the nursery blue and bought him little cars and trucks. Meanwhile, a new specialist told us that we should go on the Internet and look for other parents dealing with Dandy-Walker. We did, and Ted found many parents in England who were dealing with the syndrome. Yet they were not only surviving, but also proudly showing off pictures of their kids. Many of these children had larger-than-normal-sized heads, but their parents saw them as nothing less than a total blessing.

"I wonder if our boy will move on to heaven or stay here and deal with his issues?" I asked Ted one night when we were cuddled up in bed.

"I think he's going to be a fighter," he replied, hugging me and our unborn baby tight. In response, our son gave us a hard kick.

"That's life—that's all you can ask for," I said, happily.

In my last trimester, Ted and I paid a visit to a neurosurgeon who gave us the first bit of good news we'd had in months. "The risk of him not surviving is no more than any other child during any normal birth," the surgeon said.

"The first doctor told us there was little hope of survival, and I've spent the last ten weeks thinking that his heart will stop beating at any moment!" I cried.

The surgeon shook his head. "There's a lot of misinformation out there about Dandy-Walker," he explained. "Your boy has an 80 percent chance of survival. I can't promise you that there won't be complications, but his heart seems very strong." An echocardiogram proved this, and we discussed surgery after birth to correct any problems. It sounds strange, but I saw this as a positive sign—to plan for anything after his birth indicated to me that my baby wasn't going to die.

Suddenly, I was very upset with our original doctors. I wondered if they realized that their patients, big and small, were vulnerable. I wondered if they even cared that Ted and I lived on their every word and clung to their every sentence. I wondered if they thought about giving people any hope when hope was actually possible. And most of all, I wondered if my boy was coming soon.

Little Brandon didn't enter the world proportionally: His head was much larger than normal. In fact, he was in the 100th percentile when it came to head size, compared to the 50th percentile of most newborns whose heads match their little bodies. Brandon was a little guy with a great big head. And we looked at that head and loved every inch of it.

"Nobody tells you about this," I sobbed to Ted while looking at our son for the first time. "They tell you that you'll love your baby. But nobody tells you that you've actually grown another heart outside of your body. And then there he is looking at you. You don't see any faults. You just look in awe." And all I could do was look, because the doctors wouldn't let me hold Brandon.

As we stood there gazing at our new son, my husband and I watched a medical team whisk our son away to the neonatal ICU. Several tests later proved that his heart was miraculously and absolutely fine, which was another blessing. Eventually, Brandon did come home—along with the news that he'd always have a cyst in his brain and a larger head, but there actually might not be developmental delays if he was monitored closely and had CAT scans every six months.

Brandon was a miracle baby, although everyone wondered how such a tiny body could deal with such a big head. But as the rest of him grew bigger and bigger, suddenly his head didn't seem so large anymore. As Ted proudly says, "He's my little eater-man. The rest of him is catching up to his head."

For the first year of his life, Brandon's biggest problem was that he couldn't lift his head up or sit up on his own. Then one perfectly normal morning, I went in to check on him as he napped … and he lifted his head off the bed and looked right at me.

My son has taught me about hope and survival. At age two, this little boy began to walk. He's still a little wobbly and grabs for the wall or me—but on many days, he's not shaky at all and will run after me screaming, "Ma! Ma!"

His physical therapist arrives once a week. The child who couldn't sit up now runs around his backyard doing his favorite therapy thing in the world: He likes to steal the therapist's pens and run away with them. Developmentally, he's right on track.

"It's amazing when there were so many things that went wrong," I marveled to Ted recently. We never think about the fact that we were advised to terminate this child. It came down to hope and faith. And I smile when I hear parents complain that their child won't sleep through the night, or how they can't go out to the movies anymore. I look at my son in amazement and thank God every single time I hear him cry. He wasn't supposed to be here.

Or was he? As I've often thought, that roller-coaster ride was just the beginning. . . .

— Inspired by Ellen from Las Vegas, Nevada

Chapter 11

The Babe and the Baby
(Featuring Angelina Jolie)

It wasn't exactly the cradle of life—instead, the baby was placed in a little plastic bucket. You see, Cambodian child care isn't like what you might find in the United States. Over there, a pail is where an infant being considered for adoption is put when it won't wake up from its nap.

"They actually poured water over him," says Oscar-winning actress Angelina Jolie, wincing as she talks about meeting the love of her life for the first time. "He stayed asleep, and the orphanage people just poured more water on his tiny head to wake him up. I couldn't believe this was happening, so I scooped him up in my arms. In that moment, Maddox opened his eyes. And then he smiled."

The woman dubbed "on the edge," "high octane," and "the ultimate wild child" sounds resoundingly different from her media image. She actually seems . . . normal. These days, Jolie is just simply someone's mother. "I've never been around children in my life. I'd never really held a baby until that moment," says Angelina. "But when my son smiled, it wasn't so much that he liked me. It was more that he was okay with me. I felt that. The fact that a child would be comfortable in my arms meant a lot to me.

"The first night for us together was just me and him, totally alone in this house in the middle of Africa where I was filming *Tomb Raider 2*," Angelina recalls. "Somehow, this baby taught me how to be his parent. He told me when he was hungry. We just kind of figured it out together." Suddenly, she didn't feel like that that girl on the edge anymore—the one who has admitted that she would cut herself with knives just to feel something. "I loved it when he peed on my costumes," she says. "I loved when he barfed on me. I loved rocking him at night. I loved it all."

Part II

Lessons on Unconditional Love

"To the world you may be one person,
but to one person you may be the world."

— Anonymous

LOVE LESSONS

21. Devotion comes when you least expect it.

22. Trust in pure motives.

23. Reliability means juggling it all for your partner when he or she drops the ball.

24. You can also remember this quote by Jimi Hollemans: *"A friend's love says, 'If you ever need anything, I'll be there.' True love says, "You'll never need anything. I'll be there.'"*

Chapter 12
Kate's Comeback

It's lucky for Cinderella that she doesn't live in modern times. If she did, she'd be looking for an SDPC (Single Desirable Prince Charming) on the Internet, or trying to find him through a series of blind dates. In this cynical world, there usually aren't three wishes or a glass slipper.

But before you nod your head in agreement, let me tell you my story. It all started 13 years ago, when I was working as an emergency medical technician in Kentucky. I decided to let my friends fix me up just one more time, and then I thought that that would be it for the rest of my lonely life.

Well, that date really *did* turn into the rest of my life. I married the man I went out with, a firefighter named Mike, a year later, and our life together really was a fairy tale. Sure, we fought from time to time over trivial daily matters, but we had the secret of how to get over the bumps in the road: We dedicated our marriage to laughter and sincere honesty. Think about it for a minute. Wouldn't those two things not only save any marriage, but maybe even save the world?

Laughter and honesty helped us deal with wild schedules, stressful jobs that involved saving lives, and finding time for each other. I called our life "an amazing, wonderful juggling act." Things got even more mixed-up—but in the most wonderful way—when our two little girls were born. I can't begin to describe them in words except to say that they're the sunshine in the private world created by Mike and me.

By now you're probably wondering, "So what's the big deal with these two?" Well, it turns out that I was a little bit heavy when I fell in love with Mike, and I continued to gain weight over the years. My body and health took a bad turn, and that's when I realized that gaining more than 100 pounds was really hurting the fairy tale. Yet Mike loved me in every incarnation, every day, in every way.

In 2001, after the birth of our second daughter, I decided that I wanted a major life change and opted for weight-loss surgery. Mike was very nervous about the love of his life undergoing such a major operation, but he knew that it wasn't his decision to make. "What can I do to help you get through it?" he asked, and I knew that there was nothing more I could ask for in a man.

During the months while I waited for my surgery, I heard my late grandmother's voice telling me that a belief in God, a belief in the ones I loved, and knowing the power of love would heal my wounds and my soul. A few weeks before the surgery, those words became even more important: On July 4, while preparing for a family picnic, my foot became weirdly numb, and the feeling spread to my leg and then to the entire left side of my body. *I must have a pinched nerve,* I thought, dismissing the strange discomfort.

Mike wasn't content to let me do a home diagnosis and insisted that I consent to medical tests. Three weeks later, I was diagnosed with multiple sclerosis (MS). When I heard the news, I had my Prince Charming by my side with his arms spread wide and his heart breaking along with mine.

"This isn't our dream," I sobbed.

"It's still better that we found each other so that we could share this together," my wonderful husband said, and he meant it.

Against my doctor's advice, I decided to proceed with the weight-loss surgery. The procedure appeared to go very well at first, and I returned to work after five weeks in bed. A few days later, I was struck with severe pain in my midsection and was rushed to the hospital. It turns out that I had a perforated bowel in one of the areas that the doctor had missed during surgery. My new doctor looked at me, a very obese woman, and said sternly, "Just don't eat so many fatty foods and it will heal." He sent me packing, while Mike pleaded with him to keep me in the hospital.

The next morning at home, I knew something was wrong, so Mike drove me back to the hospital. It turns out that I had an internal infection and only would have lived a few days longer if we'd ignored it. Emergency surgery followed, and as I was wheeled away on the gurney once again, I prayed, "Please God, just let me live."

Before I reached the operating room, I kissed Mike good-bye for what I thought would be the last time. "I love you, and tell my babies I love them, too," I said. "Please go to the chapel and pray, honey. Remember what Grandma always said."

Thanks to the incredible skills of my surgeon and those prayers, I lived . . . but our family wasn't out of the woods just yet. I'd lost seven units of blood, which was a lot considering that the human body only holds nine units. This meant another surgery, and Mike visited that chapel again. Yet he didn't miss a beat at home, sending our older daughter off for her first day of school. He did the laundry, visited me, coordinated sitters, and cooked dinner. It turns out that firefighters are heroes in many ways. So many times Mike could have turned around and said, "So long. I just can't take this anymore." Instead, he treated every hurdle like just another day in the trenches. His war was to fight for the family he loved so dearly. Surrender simply wasn't an option.

Finally, I was sent home, but I had great trouble walking. Most of the time it happened at night when I felt these vicious leg tremors. Mike would simply rise at 3 A.M. with me, and then he'd carry me to the bathroom while teasing, "You women just love to be carried over the threshold." Despite the heartbreaking situation, I had to smile.

I recovered, knowing that our love had been reinforced tenfold over those two years of medical emergencies and five subsequent surgeries along with therapy for MS. Yes, there have been periods of difficulty when it comes to walking or seeing. Do I complain? Of course I do when I'm alone. But I know what I know, which is that I'm an incredibly lucky woman to have married this man. I just hope one person can hear my story, especially someone who says, "I can't do this." *Yes, you can.*

People ask how I stay so positive. Sure, things have been difficult for my family, but we're a lot luckier than most. Plus, I know that there's a big plan for everything. By the way, I've lost 175 pounds since this ordeal began, which has helped immensely with the MS therapy. My formerly size-30 figure is now a size 4. I'm able to chase my husband and children around the backyard, which is my way of living happily ever after. And my prince is still right by my side.

— Inspired by Kate from Lexington, Kentucky

LOVE LESSONS

25. Elation comes in many forms.

26. Forget diamonds, forget flowers, what women really want is for men to . . .

Chapter 13

Get Real
(Featuring Kathy Griffin)

Comedian Kathy Griffin says that the most wonderful words a man can say to her aren't "I love you":

"Once I had a boyfriend who said the most magical, romantic words that any woman has ever heard. He looked me deeply in the eyes and said, 'Babe, you look good without makeup.' A few months later he also said, 'And honey, I also love to watch you eat.' I had to think to myself, *This one is a keeper."*

Chapter 14

The Teacher Who Learned Everything

What can be said about Chuck? How can you sum up a man who lived his life honestly believing that he'd never met a stranger? People don't celebrate men like Chuck, because he never starred in a movie or ran for public office. There was nothing large or showy to celebrate: His name wasn't in the paper, and he didn't have the key to any city. He was just an "ordinary" man. It's funny that we don't celebrate the ordinary—especially when it can be quite *extra*ordinary.

Chuck preferred to live a simple life as a journey lineman at a utility company and, in typical fashion, he took enough pride in the job to devote 24 years of his life to his work. That's not exactly common in an age of giving up the first time a job gets rough. Chuck *never* gave up.

It's common to think that a man like this probably spent his nights in front of a TV set watching sports. (Why do we look at people and fill in the blanks when we truly have no idea what goes on in their lives?) In fact, Chuck actually spent his free time doing quiet things that spoke volumes: He was a faithful blood donor, collected money for diabetes research, and built Habitat for Humanity houses for those less fortunate.

Now, Chuck wasn't a saint—he simply knew that no one could collect all of life's riches without spreading them around a bit. That's why every December he'd help the local churches set up their Christmas trees. If there was someone in town who needed to move but didn't have the strength to load up their things or the money to hire a service, Chuck would show up on their driveway. "I heard you needed a little help," he'd say. You get the picture.

Anyway, I'm a local teacher who knew Chuck when we were both in high school. I thought he was cute, but nothing much ever came of it. Years later, I wasn't thinking of Chuck at all when I ended what I thought was the love affair of my lifetime. "I'm not getting serious with anyone for a long, long time," I vowed. "My heart is just too raw."

The community that Chuck served all those years saw it differently: Some well-meaning neighbors decided that the least I could do was spend a day with a man who rarely took time off for himself. I decided to go with him on a 19-mile hike to a place called Gregory Bald in the Cades Coves of Tennessee. Many women would balk at all that physical exercise on a date, not to mention the sweat involved, but I didn't care—after all, this wasn't a date. I was *not* getting into a relationship, because my heart was worn out (and so were my feet after this walk).

Nevertheless, on the way down the mountain, as hard as I tried to deny it, I knew that Chuck was "The One." He'd already figured that out about me on the way *up* the mountain.

In the weeks that followed, Chuck would drop by my school on the way to work to leave me "good morning" notes. This led to his stopping by with doughnuts for all the hardworking teachers.

And the day always ended with a little note, card, or flower on my desk.

When my classroom embarked on a planting project, Chuck was happy to build the dirt beds for the kids. He became such a presence in that classroom that the kids started calling him "Mr. Chuck"—and 11 of those same students came to our wedding the following year. Our daughter, Becky, was born soon after, and despite the fact that I'm a teacher, it was Chuck who taught her the most important life lesson: how important it is to lend a hand to friends. He included strangers in that group, telling his daughter that if you helped a stranger, there was a very good chance that person would then become a friend.

Becky would watch her daddy put up the Christmas tree at the church and say, "It's our 'Merry Christmas' to everybody." And during one especially joyous holiday season, Chuck, Becky, and I went to a concert, all three holding hands throughout the entire show. Since Chuck never left a job unfinished, that January he decided that it was only right to help take down the Christmas wreaths that he'd put up in December. Some were high up on houses, and he certainly didn't want anyone getting hurt going up there on a rickety ladder. Chuck knew that old people tended to attempt chores like that and broke their hips in the process.

When he went back to work, he saw that one wreath had been left up about 30 feet in the air, which was no problem for a man quite familiar with the necessary equipment. Putting his large truck in gear, he jumped into the bucket that was linked to a large metal arm that could reach the sky. Pushing the remote buttons, he rode up to the wreath to get the job done. That's when the bucket suddenly jolted, causing Chuck to fall to the ground. He was killed instantly.

The accident happened in front of all his co-workers, many of whom Chuck had helped in one way or another. The men stood in stunned silence because there was nothing they could do—except witness what had happened to their friend as a result of his final act of kindness.

Chuck's community was left with one question: Why? And his family was left with one question: Why us? I tell friends that this should never have happened, and that only God knows why it did. Chuck left behind a 16-year-old son from his first marriage, and a 6-year-old daughter from his second who's struggling to figure out why her daddy can't tuck her in at night.

There are days when I know that the love God gave us is the only thing that gives me the strength to go on. Chuck was my lover, my confidant, my soul mate, and my best friend. My only solace is that maybe he was needed somewhere else, and Chuck always answered a call of need.

Little Becky is a lot like her father: She's never met a stranger, and she can talk until the cows come home. Last year, she donated all $25 of her birthday money to the American Diabetes Foundation. Making Mommy laugh is Becky's job these days, which was also something that her daddy took to heart. At night, when the house is quiet, my daughter calls me into her room for a "Squeaky Story," which is something that Chuck taught her. "There's a big purple bug who lives in our front yard. He's not always here, but he goes on many adventures," Chuck would tell her.

He also taught her something that Becky doesn't understand yet, but she will someday: "Look closely at life, honey," Chuck used to tell his daughter. "Life is so very beautiful."

— **Inspired by Julie from Knoxville, Tennessee**

LOVE LESSONS

30. True love never really forgets, because it dwells somewhere deep inside.

31. Even in the toughest times, it takes just a minute or two to celebrate your blessings.

Chapter 15

Find Your Own Theme Song

Let's begin in April of 1998, when my family and I sat in the audience of a Jim Brickman concert. During the performance, his friend Anne Cochran sang a song called "After All These Years," while Jim accompanied her on the piano. As I looked across the row, I noticed that the song had brought all the members of my family to tears. As Anne softly sang, "After all these years, we still have each other. You're still around—and I'm still here," I whispered, "Grandma and Grandpa," to my husband through a veil of tears.

My grandparents, Simon and Caroline, were approaching their 50th wedding anniversary, and most of us thought it would be their last. You see, my grandmother had just been diagnosed with a rare form of cancer. She'd survived a surgery in January but was fighting as hard as she could to make it through several months of grueling chemotherapy—all the while knowing that there was no cure or even adequate long-term treatment for her.

"If I only had one wish, it would be that I'd live to see our 50th anniversary," she'd told my grandfather in her trademark scratchy voice. Grandma was determined, and so was our family. We wanted to make that anniversary a special one that they wouldn't forget.

The first step was trying to find a copy of "After All These Years." I e-mailed Jim's office, praying that my message wouldn't be tossed into a pile of unanswered fan mail. To my surprise, I received a message a few days later with a note saying that Jim's office would happily send us a copy of the song.

Meanwhile, my grandmother finished chemotherapy in June, just in time to recover for the anniversary. On a cool summer night, the entire family gathered at my grandparents' tiny house for a little surprise party.

"I want you to listen to the words of this song," I told them. As the final notes lingered in the air, it was my grandfather who had tears rolling down his face while my strong grandma just proudly held his hand. She'd made it—not only to the anniversary, but also through all the years of happiness with the man she loved. However, their special memories were soon overshadowed by the return of the cancer later that summer. The doctors said, "There are no further treatments."

During the next six months, whenever my grandmother was in pain, she'd implore the family to "play my song. It reminds me of life, not death." She finally passed away the following spring.

Today, we still hear that song on the radio, and it always makes us smile because it continues to remind us of life. It reminds my grandfather of the 50 wonderful years of love and happiness he had with his wife and the celebration she lived long enough to see.

As for me, I've only been married for a short while, but I hope and pray that 50 years from now, my husband and I can play that same song at our own party.

— Inspired by Laura from Grafton, Vermont

LOVE LESSONS

32. You have to accept life's twists and turns.

33. As the beautiful Audrey Hepburn once said, "The best thing to hold on to in life is each other."

Chapter 16

My Other Children

I stood in my kitchen and took a deep breath amid the chaos. It was the Tuesday before Thanksgiving and my "To Do" list was several pages long. On the plus side, the turkey was defrosting, the cranberries were in the fridge, and there was enough pie filling to feed a proverbial army. *This is my favorite holiday,* I thought.

As the crisp fall air flowed into the room from a lone window that was open just a little, I could smell that deliciously smoky air that comes when fireplaces start burning again in my little Arkansas town.

There were other reasons to feel especially blessed this year. After painful years of battling with infertility, soul-destroying doctor's visits, and little hope being handed my way, I'd finally heard the words that I'd been dreaming of since I was a little girl: "You have a reason to be very thankful this Thanksgiving," said my slightly amazed gynecologist. "You're pregnant. My heartiest congratulations!"

"I just can't believe it," I'd whispered, wiping away tears that had been on deck for several years. I'd never thought that I'd be able to have a child—after all, the doctors were less than encouraging. My body was simply not cooperating: My first pregnancy was an ectopic one, and I lost my right tube during an emergency surgery.

"At best, you have a 50 percent chance of conceiving," the ER doc had told me. I'd taken a deep breath, and then made a life-changing decision at that moment: I wasn't going to be one of the hopeless, but would remain utterly and amazingly hopeful.

"Well, then, I'll concentrate on the good 50 percent and try to forget about the bad," I'd said defiantly.

Now pregnant, I passed Thanksgiving in a whirlwind of congratulations, and that holiday was followed by the happiest Christmas of my life. Naturally, I was nervous when it came time to have an ultrasound, but my doctor's smiling face greatly encouraged me. "Everything is great," he said. "You're one of the lucky ones."

My husband and I did things we never thought we'd be able to do, including checking out cribs on the Internet and buying those silly baby-name books. Our baby was so very special, in every single way, and I couldn't wait to tell the story to this little boy or girl. I knew that many children weren't wanted, but our baby would know all about the longing, the waiting, the anticipation, and the pure bright love I felt to the center of my being with every single kick.

Always the domestic type, I was in the kitchen one morning cooking scrambled eggs when I felt a sharp pain in the center of my abdomen. "Honey! Oh my God!" I cried, knowing that it was too soon for our precious baby to come into the world, but holding on to the hope of the good 50 percent.

The rest was a blur, including the ambulance in the driveway, the blink-and-you'd-miss-it drive to the hospital, and the decision to transport me to a larger hospital because our local one didn't have the advanced technology that the baby and I needed.

Emergency surgery followed, and then came the worst possible news: I'd lost the baby due to another ectopic pregnancy. I almost died, and during several tense days in the hospital, my husband sat right by my side praying for my life. As my prognosis improved, I remained flat on my back in that hard hospital bed thinking about fate.

As devastated as I was about the baby, I still clung to the good 50 percent. "God was on my side—I could easily be in heaven," I told relatives who were amazed at my positive outlook.

Over the next few weeks, life went on as it always does. I was sent home from the hospital and basked in my husband's love. Thoughtful neighbors stopped by with casseroles and dinners, always careful to avoid the topic of babies or children or any bad news whatsoever. Of course they didn't want to cause me more pain, but I thought it was odd that they didn't want to *really* talk to me.

At the local store, the neighbors would speak in hushed tones and whisper how sad it was that "the poor thing lost two of her babies." They murmured that they couldn't stand that kind of pain and hugged their children tighter when they came home from school, as if my loss made them feel even luckier.

After time had passed, I thought it was indeed very strange that no one wanted to hear a story that I was longing to tell. "I think that people should know about ectopic pregnancies," I told those who would listen. "They're not only devastating, but can be life threatening. Sure, my life was spared, but I just want to make sure that others aren't lost because they're unaware," I continued, knowing that if I helped one woman realize that a sharp pain during pregnancy could mean that her life was in danger, well, then my sweet baby and I were doing something good.

At home on those quiet days, I still have moments where the sadness of losing both babies creeps up my body, reaches my throat, and then almost suffocates me. I try as hard as possible during those moments to open my kitchen window, take a deep breath of fresh air, and focus on the love and support I've found in my husband. He's not only cared for my physical needs, but he's also cared for and nurtured my emotional needs. He doesn't tell me to move on—he lets me stay in place if that's what I need.

I've also discovered something else about myself: I'm a survivor. I know that I was tested and I didn't give in. It was my lifelong dream to become a mother, but I've decided that maybe God has other plans for me. I live a happy and fulfilling life focusing again on the good 50 percent. Oh, and I've been blessed with little ones of the four-legged variety who don't look like me or my husband, thank goodness. Our 12-year-old Siamese cat, Thumper, is a true original, as is our Boston terrier puppy, Jase. They're not children, but, boy, do they fill a house with love.

On the hard days, I look across the table at my husband, who's a man of his word. On our wedding day, he vowed to love me for better or for worse and in sickness and health. He has indeed done just that.

— Inspired by Sylvia from Batesville, Arkansas

Part III

Lessons on Romantic Love

"We sat side by side by the
morning light and looked out at the future together."

— Brian Andres

34. Even the mundane can be pretty magical.

35. And the magical never gets mundane.

Chapter 17

Quickies

(Featuring Brad Pitt, Julia Roberts, Denzel Washington, Barbra Streisand, and more)

Q. What is your idea of the ideal day with your mate?

Brad Pitt, speaking about wife Jennifer Aniston: "I don't know if people would find our lives that exciting. Jen and I just like to stay home, maybe order out for a pizza or some Mexican food. It sounds simple, but we love it. We like the peaceful moments. We like nothing more than a lazy summer day with the dog on the porch."

Barbra Streisand, speaking about husband James Brolin: "My favorite time is Sunday mornings in bed watching the political shows under the covers [together]."

Q: What's the most unusual thing you've done with your main squeeze?

Jennifer Aniston: "Well, Brad needed to be bald for the movie *Fight Club*, so I shaved his head! Maybe I have inner-hairdresser tendencies. I tell my friend Chris who cuts my hair, 'Give me a station. I'll make some tip money.' Brad said I did a very good job on him."

Q: What's the most romantic thing you and your mate have done?

Melanie Griffith, on husband Antonio Banderas: "Antonio took me to Paris. We made love several times, and then we went home."

Heather Locklear, on husband Richie Sambora: "Richie and I will meet at a hotel in New York for about two hours. We call this 'rendezvousing.' It's not a surprise because we plan this stuff. One time, he helicoptered in from New Jersey, and I was waiting. You have to make these small gestures! Seriously, he is a wonderful man. I get notes from my husband all the time: He'll write, 'I'm really proud of you,' or 'I'm supporting you,' or 'I love you so much.' We're coming up on our ten-year anniversary, and I've saved all those notes for a decade."

Q: How did you almost blow it big time?

Michael Chiklis: "I met my future wife, Michelle, at a party that neither of us wanted to go to. It was the classic story of being dragged there by your friends. The moral of the story is if you're feeling bad and don't want to go out and meet anyone, and your friends scream at you to go, then get your butt off the couch and get out of the house! I did that and met my soul mate. I met a woman who is all the things your wife should be: your friend, your confidante, your lover, and your partner. I can't even imagine my life if I didn't go to that party."

Q: What was the most difficult time for you?

Denzel Washington: "We were poor when I first started acting. Very poor. I remember my wife, Pauletta, and I lived in an apartment where the floors were so slanted that we'd wake up and our furniture had rolled over to one side of the place. Did she complain? No. We just laughed and were thankful that we were together. And we counted every blessing and victory. I remember when I got the job on *St. Elsewhere*—it gave us the opportunity to buy our first car. That was major."

Q: How do you make it work?

Julia Roberts, on husband Danny Moder: "I found someone who brings out the best in me. He brought a real ease to my life. It's all about finding that balance in your life."

Q: What's your favorite trait about your mate?

Jennifer Aniston: "It's so nice to be married to someone you like a lot. Brad's a nice man; he's considerate; I'm just so impressed with him. How could I not love him?"

Q: How do you keep the passion alive?

Goldie Hawn, discussing partner Kurt Russell: "To be honest, I feel sexier now in this relationship with Kurt than when I was younger and first met him. Sexuality grows and develops with us as we get older. The important thing is not to dwell on this obsession with youth. Youth only works for so long as an elixir to turn someone on. You must get very real with your partner and know what's underneath your love. I found that it's about energy, which is not something that only the young have. Energy at any age is an incredible turn-on. We've never lost that energy for each other."

Q: What was the worst date of your life?

George Clooney: "I took this girl to the prom and I didn't remember her address to take her home. Well, she wouldn't give it to me because she didn't want the date to end. I ended up getting stopped by the police for speeding and I explained the situation to the officer. He looked up her address for me so I could drop her off and call it a night. I love our friends in blue!"

LOVE LESSONS

36. Trust someone else's instincts.

37. Dogs aren't just man's best friend—they're also pretty good for women, too.

Chapter 18

Puppy Love

Our matchmaker's name is Jake. He has black curly hair that covers his tiny body, four legs, and enough instinctual intelligence to solve most of the world's love problems.

Jake is a cute miniature poodle who moved into the apartment next door and immediately developed a crush on me. It was serious because each time I opened the door, he'd be right there in the hallway just waiting to run inside my place for a quick date. He was smart enough to figure out that a woman needs special quality time with her "man," so at night we'd go out on the deck of our building and watch the beautiful Seattle sun blaze away until it set for the day. We were a "coosome twosome," Jake and me . . . until one evening when we became a threesome.

"There you are," said a man's voice. "I've been looking all over for you."

The human's name was Bruce, and he was worried about his dog, who kept disappearing on a daily basis. Jake didn't look too nervous about the repercussions—after all, he was a canine on a mission. And with a furious wag of his tail, he moved over and let Bruce sit down next to me.

Glancing at Jake, I suddenly realized that he didn't really have a crush on me. It was almost as if he knew that his owner would like me even better, and someone had to do something to get this relationship off the ground. At that moment, I had a strange feeling that Jake had been "suggesting" for a long time that his handsome owner join our evening dates.

Bruce didn't seem to mind, because he introduced himself, and we began a lively discussion about the life of our pint-sized, furry host. So after that night, Jake and I expanded our group, waiting up on the deck until Bruce could join us after work for our evening ritual.

One night the humans decided to do something quite decadent. "Would you like to ditch the pup and go out for dinner alone?" Bruce suggested.

Feeling a twinge of guilt, I knew that I had to ask permission. "Do you mind?" I turned to ask Jake, but he'd mysteriously disappeared for the night.

"He must have a date, too. There's a hot beagle who lives down the hall," joked my future husband.

"Who is she? I think we should check her out. Is she good enough for our Jake?" I teased.

Months later, Bruce and I were lying in each other's arms with guess who at our feet? We feel very blessed in our love for each other—and our love for this tiny dog, our matchmaker.

I believe that this little poodle is actually a very old soul. There are so many times when I wish he could talk, because I can see the wisdom in his warm brown eyes. It's obvious that he was looking out for Bruce and instinctively knew that the three of us would be perfect together. It's funny that humans often miss all the basic signs that animals have no trouble spotting.

Thanks to Jake, our happy family is celebrating 8 years together this fall (or 72 years of bliss in dog years). By the way, dogs aren't called man's best friend for nothing—but what they don't get credit for is knowing how to fill a woman's heart, too.

— Inspired by Olivia from Seattle, Washington

LOVE LESSONS

38. Courtesy matters.

39. Empathy works the best.

40. Respect means never leaving a breakup note.

Chapter 19

The Man and the Post-it
(Featuring Ron Livingston)

He wants the women of the world to know he's sorry—he's living with the pain, and he's lamenting. Yes, actor Ron Livingston played the man who broke up with Carrie Bradshaw on *Sex and the City* by leaving a Post-it note on her computer after they'd just made mad, passionate love. *The cad!*

Sure, his character, a handsome love-'em-and-leave-'em type named Jack Berger, scampered away in shame, but only after posting news of their lack of a future together by writing: "I can't. I'm sorry. Don't hate me."

Livingston says, "How can I explain myself to the millions of women out there? I feel like I should wear a sign that says, 'Hi. Sorry about the Post-it thing,'" He continues, "Right after it aired, I couldn't go anywhere without getting lots of dirty looks. There were some very angry women out there. I felt like saying, 'Do you people know truth from reality? It's just a show.' Even very upscale women would stare at me like, 'You scumbag.' But then I was surprised at how quickly it blew over. I guess women are very quick to forgive," says this handsome man with a deep sigh.

For those women who can't forgive him, perhaps there's a balm: Livingston has been dumped in the past in ways that have hurt him more than a Post-it ender. "The worst for me was when a girl once tried to let me down easy," he says. "She said, 'Listen, it's not you. It's me.' That sucks. Boy, does that suck. I'd rather she set my car on fire."

LOVE LESSONS

41. Even if you fumble the first time
at love, you can still score a major win.

42. What's old can be renewed again.

Chapter 20

The Boomerang

My love story started back in 1986 at Jack London High School in Missouri. It was the fall of my junior year when I had a class with Paul. There was an instant attraction on my part—in fact, I acted like I was in the first grade. I knew his friend Greg, so I had him give Paul a note I'd written. Needless to say, we fell in love, and I truly believed that we had a future. But he broke my heart in the fall of 1987 when he notified me, "I just don't think I love you anymore."

I was devastated, but I slowly came back to life and graduated from London High. After a few years at technical college, I decided that I had to move on with my life and start again on the emotional front. Around that time, I met someone and married him, and we went on to have three children who are my life. But I slowly started noticing the signs that I wasn't in a healthy relationship—for example, my husband was a very controlling man who soon became both emotionally and physically abusive.

I thought, *If I could only change something in myself, then maybe that would make him happy.* But nothing made him happy—nothing. During the bleakest times when I was in serious pain, I'd let my mind wander back to my handsome football hero, Paul. At least my husband could never take those memories away from me.

Even though I never talked about Paul, which would have proved dangerous in my house, I did run into his family from time to time, and they told me that he was doing well. That made me happy, since at least one of us deserved as much.

In the summer of 2002, I was thrown down a staircase. Black and blue, but not defeated, I finally found the courage to stand up—literally—and tell my husband, "I've had enough. Your children can't think this is a normal relationship. If you don't get out, I'm going to press charges."

He cried, promised me that he'd change, and begged my forgiveness for the millionth time. But I knew that his anger would never change, and that sent me to an attorney's office. On that long road to divorce, I kept to myself, healed both emotionally and physically, and found joy in surfing the Internet. Then one sunny spring morning, I received an e-mail. "Hello," it said. "How are you, Karen? Did you know that we're having our 15-year high school reunion next year . . . can you believe it's been 15 years already? Your friend, Paul."

My heart was in my mouth, my blood was tingling, and I was in absolute heaven.

We began to correspond, and Paul told me that he'd never married—of course he'd dated around, but it had never led to anything serious. I didn't tell him about my divorce at first, pretending to be a happily married mother. (You can call it pride or stupidity.) Then one night, I poured out my story to him, and he said, "Get off the computer right now. I want to call you." We talked for so long that my sleepy six-year-old son finally came into my room and asked if he could have doughnuts for breakfast.

Paul didn't want to end our conversation. "You know, I really think . . . ," he began, before his voice trailed off. It was never easy for Paul to put his feelings into words. "I, uh, think that you're my soul mate," he finally blurted out. "I *never* stopped loving you, Karen. I'm so sorry for saying those hurtful things all those years ago. I was just so scared because I felt something deeply for the first time in my life."

At that point, I burst into tears, and my son just looked at me in the most befuddled way. "Mommy, don't cry. I'll have cereal," he said.

Paul and I continued to correspond for months, but we didn't see each other. "I want your divorce to be final so that we can have a clean slate," he explained during one of our nightly marathon phone calls.

On Valentine's Day 2003, my divorce did become final, and Paul and I met for the first time in 15 years. It was magic: He hadn't changed, but everything else had. He proposed that summer, asking me by my maiden name if I'd marry him. Of course, I cried. Paul has shown me what love is, and not once has he lifted a finger to me except to stroke my cheek.

— **Inspired by Karen from Kansas City, Missouri**

Chapter 21

Chocolate Therapy
(Featuring Brittany Murphy)

We've all heard about the different stages of grief after the death of a loved one. It follows that there are similar stages when it comes to breaking up with a boyfriend or girlfriend. Actress Brittany Murphy, has been linked with

Eminem and Ashton Kutcher and only recently ended an engagement, is happy to be a life coach on this subject. "I really do believe there are different stages. Let's list them, because we've all been through these stages and it helps to identify your progress," she insists.

"First, there is denial," she explains. "That's followed by step two, which is tears.

"Step three is chocolate, chocolate, and more chocolate. It's definitely the best step and worth it if you mix up candy with cookies and then ice cream," she advises.

"Step four is ambivalence—and you should start working out to get rid of that chocolate. Finally, the last step to healing is when you get your fight up. After that, you should be back on your feet again and, hopefully, you've learned a life lesson without gaining too much weight!"

LOVE LESSONS

45. In times of despair, the heart can find repair.

46. Even if your mind is screaming *no, no, no*, you have to give yourself a chance.

Chapter 22

Why Now?

"A deck party?!" I exclaimed. "You want *me* to celebrate the beginning of summer?" Certainly, my friend Rosie had a screw loose. There was no one on this planet who was in less of a party mood than I was.

Eight years of hell and now I'm free, I thought. After more than 2,900 days in a physically and emotionally abusive marriage, I'd ultimately hit rock bottom. It still amazed me that the reason I was finally able to separate from my spouse wasn't thanks to our nightmare marriage, but because *he* came home one day and simply informed me that he'd become involved with someone else—and they were in love!

"Lucky girl," I spat to my friends, who had begged me to leave for years. Finally able to find the strength, I packed up my two children, speed-dialed a good lawyer, and moved into an apartment with a roommate. It certainly wasn't easy financially, but we were free.

Freedom didn't mean that I was in the mood to go have a good time, however. It was enough that I was now leading a healthy life, and it consisted of getting through the day, helping the kids, and maybe watching a little TV if I had a spare moment. Void of extra energy, I flopped down on my couch when Rosie mentioned the idea of a neighborhood deck party. Unfortunately, she also bugged me to the point where I couldn't stand it anymore and promised to put in an appearance. *I'll go for a few minutes and then be back in time for David Letterman,* I resolved.

"Maybe you'll meet a new man," Rosie offered.

"Oh, that's just what I need in my life: another guy," I said, rolling my eyes. This was her most absurd idea yet.

The night of the big event, I dug out a casual yellow sundress, managed to zip myself up, and walked over to the wooden deck where the party was in full bloom. Brightly colored lanterns were everywhere, drinks were flowing, and the smell of chicken on the grill made my mouth water. *Maybe this won't be so bad,* I thought.

Waving to my friends, my hand stopped when I spotted Alex, the nice man from across the street. The two of us had given each other friendly waves over the last few weeks, which prompted Rosie to give me the 411 on Alex. He was in the process of separating from his wife of 19 years, who'd informed him that she'd met someone over the Internet and was thus abruptly ending their union to run off with this orthodontist from Ohio. I listened to this story with disgust and made another mental note for the book I might write one day called *Why I Will Never Fall for Anyone Ever Again.*

Yet falling for and talking to someone were two different things, so I was curious when Alex approached me to say hello. "I thought I might introduce myself because I've seen you around the neighborhood. I'm Alex," said the handsome, slightly balding man in jeans and a crisp blue shirt.

"I'm Vickie, and I don't know why I'm here," I blurted out, nervously twisting one hand with the other. It had been so long since I'd been to a party, let alone talked to an attractive man.

"Well, why don't we get a drink, and we'll figure out why we're both here," Alex offered. It was then that I realized that he also seemed a little bit shy and nervous.

Over a beer, Alex and I did the requisite small talk, covering the weather and where we grew up. A soft drink later, we progressed to jobs and favorite movies. Digging into that grilled chicken, we moved on to more in-depth conversation including recent breakups, our kids, and what we really wanted out of life.

"I don't think I've ever had a real relationship," I found myself confessing. "It's just been one big void for me."

Unlike many other men who like to clam up when the conversation turns to love, Alex poured out his feelings: "I think that there are ways a man should treat a woman he cares for deeply," he said, explaining that "the little things are as important as the big ones: Breakfast in bed, flowers, a little loving note—is that asking too much?"

I'd asked much less of my marriage, yet I'd somehow ended up with deep wounds. However, being a romantic at heart, I dared to wonder aloud about the kind of relationship I wanted as a young woman: "Why can't you tell someone you love that you do love them? And why not tell them every single day?"

Alex took it from there. "I think you should always kiss the person good-bye before you leave the house. Oh, and you should never go to bed mad at each other. I think I heard that on *Oprah.*"

I laughed, admitting that I'd seen that very episode myself. I continued our discussion: "Maybe I've been silly about this in the past, but as long as the other person wants to work at the relationship, I've always thought that things would be okay," I shared.

"But there are times when you have to leave," Alex gently said. I had no idea at the time that he knew about my past from a few nosy neighbors who meant well, but had spilled all to him.

Before I knew it, hours had passed. I couldn't believe that I was sitting next to a man whose very being seemed to emit a warm glow. Sneaking shy glances when I thought he wasn't looking, I saw compassion and comfort. Then I'd end up scolding myself: *You don't know this man. You can't trust him.* I longed to give Alex the benefit of the doubt, but I wasn't sure if I was just being foolish again when it came to men.

I can talk to this guy about anything and nothing at all, I realized, as we sat on his porch swing until three in the morning. Floating home in complete awe, I thought hard about what had happened, and my brain went into shock mode. My emotions were mixed and my stomach was jumping. *How can I possibly trust another man again? Aren't they all this nice in the beginning?* My mind raced.

But is it possible that there's another person out in the world who's truly meant for me and my children? Could there be someone who would stand next to us and remain patient while we healed?

My biggest question revolved around the timing of it all: *How is it possible that at the lowest point of my entire life, this wonderful person suddenly turns up? Why now?*

I finally decided that even if I never saw Alex again, I'd always have those few hours that restored my faith in the possibility that kindness existed.

As the weeks went on and summer turned into a chilly fall, Alex and I continued to have our late-night talks while rocking on the porch swing. Our meetings weren't planned: He'd be out taking a walk or I'd be spotted tossing out the trash—and we always ended up chatting up a storm. The very randomness of it all made me feel more at ease.

Even though I wasn't one to embrace old sayings, one kept going through my mind as I sat on that swing: "When a door closes, a window opens." I reasoned that for some people, it takes a long time for that window to open, but for the lucky, it only takes a matter of moments—or one really good deck party.

Many months later, I stopped having nightmares about my past, and my marriage became more and more distant in my mind. Those feelings of insignificance and that bottomless void in my soul were filled with warmth; a new strength; and complete, unconditional love from a man who asked for nothing in return except a few minutes on that swing each night (weather permitting). The most difficult time of my life had ended, and the most rewarding part was just beginning. . . .

One day Alex greeted me at the door of my home. His divorce was final, and he had one simple question that couldn't wait for the swing later that night: "What are you doing the rest of your life?"

Before I could answer, he dropped down on one knee and presented me with a lovely diamond ring. "I'd like you to spend it with me," he said.

I could think of nothing better. But my tears didn't begin to flow until I learned moments later that Alex had just returned from meeting with my elderly parents and asking permission for their daughter—mother of two, survivor of much—to join him in a loving marriage. It's those little things that make Alex so special.

Today, I don't question good fortune or happy days anymore. Destiny works in mysterious ways—who am I to wonder why?

— Inspired by Cheryl from Indianapolis, Indiana

Chapter 23

Dancing Queen
(Featuring Michael Douglas and Catherine Zeta-Jones)

On their first date, Michael Douglas had an unusual proposition for Catherine Zeta-Jones. He didn't want to get her into the bedroom—instead, he pointed to the bathroom and said, "Prove it to me."

The entire night, Catherine had bragged to Michael that she was a fantastic tap dancer. He wasn't sure if he believed her, so late in the evening, he finally asked her to do a number for him. There was just one problem, and it had a very expensive price tag attached to it: Michael was worried about his house. He implored, "Cat, just don't ruin my hardwood floors because I've just had them redone. But I do have a bathroom with hard ceramic tiles."

Catherine recalls responding, "This is too weird! I'm not tap dancing in your bathroom! Where are you going to sit—on the toilet? Are you going to lean on the tub and watch me?"

It turns out that that was exactly what Michael planned on doing. He sat down on the ceramic throne and tossed the throw rug into the tub. That's when Catherine took one look at him and decided that she would tap her way into his heart. Little did she know that Michael's own feelings were already doing a two-step.

"It must have been love, because I tapped my little heart out that night," she recalls, touching a big, jeweled "C" and "M" shield that dangles from her neck. She calls it "my Michael and Catherine necklace."

Of course, the rest is history, and the lovebirds have two beautiful children and homes around the world. As she says, "We are so happy, and we look out for each other. As for the secret to our love, I don't have all the answers. I do know that I never get off the phone with him without saying 'I love you.'

"We're the kind of people who wear our hearts on our sleeves," she says.

So what if they're designer sleeves?

LOVE LESSONS

50. At every age, you might listen
to your elders for a second.

51. Love truly is a shield from harm—
but if not, a good medallion will also do.

Chapter 24

Mother Knows Best

"The Moms," as we call them, began their daily "advice
column" when I was 10 and Christy was 11. We lived in a
small Illinois town, and our mothers were the best of
friends. I think there was a secret conspiracy from the
beginning for this girl and me to end up together. After
all, the Moms used to sit on their front porches and say,
"One day, when you kids get married . . ."

"Ick," I'd say, pulling away on my little red bike—which was the manly thing to do when you're ten.

"I'm going to marry Captain Kangaroo," said Christy, tossing a wad of gum at me when no one was looking.

Despite that type of taunting, we became fast friends and were fairly inseparable during our adolescence. Around the age of 15, my family moved to Texas, and it looked as though our mothers' conspiracy wouldn't work out as planned. I pretty much shut Christy out of my head, although we did become pen pals.

The Texas days came to a close and my family moved to central Florida. While our communication became a little less consistent, somehow when Christy and I did talk, it was like we picked up where we left off every time. Then something happened that left me pretty depressed: Christy went to France for a year after high school. I wasn't sure why I was so sad, but I think I knew that I was losing a part of me that had just always been there.

Despite outrageous phone bills, we were able to keep in touch. Our friendship miraculously stayed very constant and secure. And, while romance never peeked into the picture, we knew that a bond existed that would never go away. Finally, I got this crazy idea that maybe, just maybe, there was something deeper than friendship developing. Yet, try as I might to convince her, she wouldn't hear of it—and I found myself in the "dumped" category although we'd never really dated. It's almost worse when your best friend breaks up with you, and the only solution was going away to college and starting a new life.

"You're still going to marry Christy someday," my mother told me.

"Mom, that's crazy!" I protested.

College brought a whole new world my way, and a lot less Christy—we talked a handful times during the entire year. But each conversation made it feel as if we'd talked for hours every day. The connection was still steadfast, and our maturing hearts seemed to beat a little closer together.

I returned home to Florida for the summer, which is when I did something that made the Moms very happy: I invited Christy to stay with my family and me for a week. I thought it would be a great time to catch up and spend some much-needed time together.

She arrived, and our time couldn't have been more beautiful. It felt like a movie, but this was real life. One night we went for a walk out on a pier that stretched into a beautiful, calm lake. The gentle breeze, the water lapping against the rocks, and the stars glistening above us seemed to whisper that we were beginning to understand what the Moms always knew.

Christy returned home, and our mothers were the first to rejoice because their little conspiracy had indeed panned out the way they'd hoped from the start. Every single time I thought of forgetting about Christy, my mother urged me to give her a call. And each time she thought about dating someone else, her mother reminded her that a really good guy was also waiting for her.

Last summer, Christy and her parents were vacationing off the coast of Florida, and my brother and I went down to join them for a weekend. This was the time for Christy to become significantly more than my girlfriend.

The day of days arrived, and I awoke with a pounding heart and sweating hands. I prayed for a beautiful amber sunset, but as the day progressed, I realized that torrential downpours rarely give way to sunsets. Around my neck hung the most important item I'd ever owned: Christy's engagement ring.

The afternoon was forced aside by evening, which gave way to even heavier rains than before. Christy and I sat on the couch watching TV, she in her unsuspecting innocence, and I with heart-wrenching anticipation. Finally, I prayed silently: *God, if you want me to ask her even with the rain, please give me a sign.* The moment I did so, she looked outside and said, "That's the most beautiful rain I've ever seen."

Nervously, I took that as a sign and announced, "Well, I'm going to the back porch to watch it." I knew that she'd follow me, and we sat on an old oak bench overlooking the choppy ocean, as sheets of rain pelted everything in sight. It was time.

I took a deep breath and told Christy a story from World War I. Now, before you pass judgment on war stories in a marriage proposal, understand that this was the story of a brave volunteer who dropped out of school to fight for our freedom. In his troop, each soldier was given a medallion that they wore everywhere they went, signifying their allegiance, even in death, to the cause. Sadly, this soldier was captured and stripped of every possession except the medallion. He escaped and was found by the French, who honored him for keeping his medallion and continuing to fight. The number one rule of his unit had been: *Never be caught without your medallion.*

As I finished the story, I reached into a pouch around my own neck and pulled out the ring. I explained that I also had a medallion that I carried with me that signified my commitment to Christy and to our love, my commitment to fight for her, to honor her, and to be faithful to her, even during the hard times. It symbolized a love that would last for all time, reserved only for her.

Christy's shocked face was by far the most priceless moment of the night. She began to laugh hysterically as I asked "the" question—and then she gave me a steady and sure "Yes." Euphoria commenced as we began screaming and rejoicing.

The first ones we told, of course, were the Moms, who each sang the same song: "We always knew it!" they rejoiced.

"I had to say yes. Captain Kangaroo wasn't available," Christy teased them.

— **Inspired by Ben from Rochester, New York**

LOVE LESSONS

52. Take a risk—even if you come off as cocky.

53. Humor, not to mention a cute smile, means that even cocky can be fun.

Chapter 25

No Bum Rap
(Featuring LL Cool J)

He's one of America's first rap stars, but LL Cool J doesn't get a bum rap in the love department. He met his wife, Symone, in the early '90s after an Easter celebration. She was standing outside church with her friends when LL, whose real name is James Todd Smith, drove up.

"Do you have a phone?" he asked the stunned Symone.

"Yes, I have a phone," she replied.

"Well, if you have a phone, then you have a number. Could you please give it to me?" LL asked.

The one whose rap moniker stems from "Ladies Love Cool James" laughs and says that it was only one special lady who interested him. The two married in 1995 and have four children.

"She's a real strong woman," LL says. "She's intuitive, and she's my best friend." And just because he comes off like a tough guy doesn't mean the actor-rapper doesn't have a soft side. Now a major sex symbol, LL says that he's romantic, but not in a Hallmark way. "There's a difference between being romantic and being overbearing. It's a fine line," he insists.

He can even illustrate: "Let's say the ladies reading this go home from work one night and they find out that their husband has a candlelight dinner prepared. That's romantic. But it can be just as romantic to say, 'Honey, let's go out to Benihana.' Sometimes you want the Benihana because too many candlelight dinners at home is a little crazy. It has to be special and not everyday to mean something," he insists.

Deep down, LL's also a romantic man. Ask him what he finds especially loving and he sighs. "I think the most romantic thing is just the tender touch of a woman who loves you. Just being that close is romantic," he reveals. "My woman can sit in my lap—we can just be having a conversation, and it's the best moment in my world.

"I can hug her for 15 seconds and that's enough to send my heart into overdrive," he says.

Chapter 26

The Predictable Man

It's funny how your best trait can often come back to haunt you. I'd describe myself as a good man who's very steady, honest, and—yes, I admit it—a tad predictable and cautious. So when it came time to propose to my true love, Donna, I sought the counsel of her sister, Joan.

I was elated when Joan told me that Donna was very much in love and absolutely ready to marry me, and she even figured that a proposal was in the near future. Joan didn't want to ruin the surprise, but she *did* want to give me a little heads-up: "She thinks you'll propose in the traditional way. She has you figured out and loves that you're so predictable," Joan informed me.

At first I was hurt—after all, who wanted to be so easy to figure out? But then I realized that this was one of the traits that Donna found dear. If only I could find a way to propose that rocked her world....

One day I was at my mother's house, and she said, "Why don't you propose at that concert you're taking Donna to? You know, the one with the romantic piano player."

I loved the idea and tried to figure out how to contact Jim Brickman. I was in luck when he made an appearance in my hometown, and I tried to ask if he'd help me pop the question to Donna at his show. Jim's tour manager, Wendy, apologetically replied, "I'm so sorry, but we can't do two proposals in one night." Undaunted, I went home and decided that I'd propose at the symphony another night. It was still good, but not as good as proposing at a concert where we could hear a song named "Destiny," which pretty much summed up my love affair with Donna.

Later that afternoon, the phone rang. It was Wendy, who asked, "Do you think you could still propose at the show?" she asked with a laugh.

"I just can't believe it," I said. "I didn't think—"

Wendy interrupted my reverie by saying that she'd leave different tickets for us that night so we'd be close to the stage. A plan was set.

Donna was in a particularly happy mood as we headed to Jim's concert, but I was a little stressed out. Fretting that she'd wonder about the ticket change, I left her in the popcorn line and snuck over to the box office to collect the new tickets. We took our seats as the moon was rising and the thin silvery clouds began to part. The yellow light from above was only blocked by the dark silhouette of the naked late-autumn trees. I couldn't believe it when I then felt something wet on my cheek. It was the shimmering, icy wonder of soft snowflakes that had begun to fall without warning.

I held the love of my life close as the snow swirled around us, and I became lost in my thoughts. Life couldn't get much better.

Donna grabbed my hand as the curtain lifted and a starry background was illuminated on the stage. A million pinpoints of light flooded the sky as Jim Brickman began to play an achingly lovely song. "How did we ever get lucky enough to have these seats?" she whispered.

"I guess we're pretty blessed," I said.

Halfway through the show, Jim stopped playing and spoke into the microphone. "I believe that there's someone here tonight who has a special question to ask a special someone," he said.

I didn't move, but the man sitting next to Donna stood up. This stranger grabbed the hand of a beautiful redhead sitting next to him and said, "I've been wanting to ask you this for a long, long time: Will you marry me?"

The woman gasped and then jumped up into his arms and said yes as the crowd greeted them with deafening applause.

"I can't believe it," Donna whispered to me. "We're sitting right next to them. Wow!" Little did she know that she was next.

At that point, Jim's singer and friend, Anne Cochran, took over the microphone. "Jim, I wonder if anyone else has a question."

The crowd became strangely silent and everyone began to look around at the other couples, wondering, *Could it be them? Could they be next?* Donna giggled in the midst of this lovefest, never imagining or even hoping that it could be her—her Ron would *never* do something like this in public.

"Well, *does* anyone else have a question?" Jim asked, thinking that perhaps I'd chickened out. But I knew that this was our time, so I raised my hand as if I were a boy in school. Realizing that this was ridiculous, I stood up and finally shouted, "Yes! I have a question, too!"

A surprised Donna could do nothing else but yank at my pants and gasp, "Sit down! What are you doing?"

I knew exactly what I was doing when I walked onstage and took the microphone from Anne, which wasn't what anyone predicted.

"What's your name?" Anne asked me, leaning into the mike I now held.

"My name is Ron, and I need to borrow this mike," I said, walking back to my seat with my heart pounding. "Donna, please stand up," I continued. Somehow my lovely girlfriend found the strength to get over her shock and actually rise. "Everybody, this is Donna," I said, and the crowd cheered. "She means everything to me. I love her very, very much."

At that point, I knelt down and looked up into my beloved's eyes. "I love you more than all the stars in the heavens. Will you marry me?"

"Oh my God! Yes!" she cried.

I almost couldn't believe it, and my hands were shaking so hard that I could barely put the ring on her finger. "I think my life with you will be filled with surprises," she whispered when Jim began to play again.

"You can count on it," I told her with a smile.

Mr. Predictable had left the building.

— Inspired by Ron from Providence, Rhode Island

Chapter 27

How Did They Pop the Question?
(Featuring Rita Wilson, John Travolta, and Paul Reiser)

Rita Wilson, on how Tom Hanks asked for her hand in marriage: "We were in the French West Indies. It was New Year's Eve, and the clock was starting to go

'10, 9, 8, 7' . . . the countdown was on. In those few seconds between seven and one, Tom said, 'I love you. Will you be my wife?' And in like a millisecond I said, 'You bet!' And we were married four months later. It was really great because I had no idea he was going to propose."

John Travolta, on his proposal to Kelly Preston: "It was midnight in the middle of a castle. I waited until the clock struck 12 and asked Kelly. What followed can only be described as projectile tears."

Paul Reiser, on asking future wife, Paula, to marry him: "It was such a big deal because I had a hard time saying the words. I just couldn't stop laughing. The whole thing just felt so weird. Asking for a hand in marriage, I felt like I was in the middle of some bad Ronald Colman movie. You have a lot to consider, like should you be down on one knee or two knees? Should knees even be involved? Those are the questions. But finally I asked, and she actually did say yes. I think at that point I got a little dizzy, but I didn't pass out. I just said, 'Really? You said yes? You have no problem with marrying me?'"

LOVE LESSONS

58. There's no such thing as a wrong number if you truly connect.

59. It's not just ET who phones and finds a home.

Chapter 28

Wrong Number

I was a nanny living in a zillion-dollar mansion in Los Angeles. After an exhausting day with two preschool boys who technically belonged to a harried movie studio executive who was also a single mother, my feet were burning. Sitting down to take my first deep breath of the day, my peace wasn't interrupted by a shrill scream or a toddler squabble, but by a ringing phone.

Oh God, don't let it wake up the kids! I worried as I made a mad grab for the receiver. I was instructed to take detailed messages for my boss, so I said, "Hello, may I help you?" sounding as professional as possible for someone who'd just dug two mushed-up crayons out of a $10,000 silk sofa.

"I'm sorry," said the deep, befuddled voice on the other end of the line. "I think I dialed the wrong number. Sorry to bother you."

I'm still not sure why I said another word and didn't just let the moment pass—but I didn't. "Don't be sorry," I said. "It's nice to talk to someone who isn't three years old."

"Your kids?" he inquired.

"Oh, no," I said. "I'm just the nanny. I moved from Denver to L.A. to take this job." I stopped there, fearful that I was telling a complete stranger my entire life story. Maybe I was a little overtired, because it wasn't like me to open up to a faceless voice on the other end of a phone line.

"No one is 'just the nanny.' It sounds like a tough job," the voice sympathized.

We spoke several minutes longer and laughed a lot. It seemed unbelievable, but I was having a wonderful time with my wrong number. It didn't even seem so odd when he called the next night and we talked again. In a matter of days, the conversations became longer and longer, and a wonderful friendship began to develop—even though it was certainly a bit unorthodox in its origin.

A cautious woman, I was a bit afraid to take things any further. It took months of calls for Morgan, the mystery caller, to convince me that we should meet in a very public place. On a cool fall day, I drove over to the Santa Monica pier, an open-air market of shops and restaurants complete with a gigantic sky-high Ferris wheel.

As an extra insurance policy, I'd brought my cousin with me just in case Morgan wasn't what he seemed or was tattooed from top to bottom or looked like someone I saw on an episode of *America's Most Wanted*. I needn't have worried: In person, Morgan was extremely good-looking, exceedingly nice, and just a normal guy who'd pressed a three instead of a two on the phone one night. It turned out to be a lucky thing.

The friendship continued when my nanny job was over and I returned home to Denver. Last summer, Morgan and I met in Las Vegas and didn't even gamble—we'd already hit a different kind of jackpot because we're completely in love with each other.

Of our fateful first discussion, Morgan and I just shake our heads. When we tell people, no one ever believes us, but we know the truth. At times, we joke about finding a copy of those phone records just to prove it to our friends.

"Everything happens for a reason," Morgan likes to say.

Oh, and we still talk on the phone because we miss each other when we're not together. He has my number, and vice versa.

— **Inspired by Marcy from Denver, Colorado**

Chapter 29

An Ode to St. Valentine
(Featuring Adam Sandler)

Adam Sandler recalls that Valentine's Day was a holiday that usually wiped the smile off his face. But the self-described "geek" says that one year his luck changed for the better.

"The most romantic thing that ever happened to me was in the third grade. I was the boy who looked geeky and never got any cards on Valentine's Day. So one depressing year, after suffering total rejection on a daily basis, I looked into that sad, empty little box taped to my desk and there was a note in there from one of the girls. She wrote, 'I don't really like you. I don't want to go out with you. I just wanted to let you know that you're okay.'

"It was better than a million 'I love you' cards."

Part IV

Lessons on Making It Work

"To me, the type of things that people do that make their lives heroic are a lot of times very small, little things that happen in the kitchen or between a husband and wife, or between them and their kids."

— Bruce Springsteen

"The bigger the fight, the better the sex."

— John Leguizamo

Chapter 30

The Wild Child

I was a real wild one in my younger years. During my sophomore year of high school, my parents pulled the plug on their own love, which sent me on a very reckless course. I'll skip the gory details, but by the time I turned 16, I was headed for total destruction—my life was fast, hard, and out of control.

By age 19, I hit the brakes. "Wild" turned into "mild," and my path suddenly became quite clear. I was ready for a brand-new start at a community college in New York City, which we'd all dubbed "The Rock." That's okay—I needed something as steady as a rock to help me find a grounded future. And love wasn't supposed to walk into my life like it did. In fact, I never saw it coming.

Only a few weeks before I met The One, I'd made a promise to myself that I wouldn't date anyone until I finished college and cleaned up my life. I even made a list of characteristics for a datable guy, and I swore not to settle for anything less than a true Prince Charming. After all, my first semester in college had already left me with a psycho who said he was in love with me after knowing me for a week, and one date I dubbed "The Vampire" because he'd only come out at night and had decided at the tender age of 24 that he'd never commit to anyone or anything.

There seemed to be only one logical solution to this mess: I'd devote myself to school and work to save up money for my future, which would certainly involve my growing old alone. However, right before the new school year began, my friend Celine called to invite me to her home in Boston for a calm, friendly gathering of pals, which included a guy she knew from a small town in Massachusetts. Hello—it was a party, and I couldn't turn it down. My new responsible self figured that school didn't start until September, and it was a weekend, so I didn't have to worry about work either. Immediately, I called my friend Nikki, who loved a party as much as I did, and we set off.

Arriving at Celine's house, I was a proud, single girl who was ready to share my horror stories if anyone asked me for them. Two minutes after I cleared the front door, I spotted Phil, Celine's small-town friend, and I realized that fate was taking over. Never one to believe in love at first sight, I nevertheless knew that I was looking into the bright eyes of my future. It wasn't just that he had strikingly handsome features, including a square jaw and chestnut hair (although that didn't hurt). The world around me simply turned into that cliché where the heroine goes weak in the knees when she locks eyes with the handsome prince. *Go slowly. You're not a wild child anymore. You're worth more than that, and he looks like he's worth more than that. And you don't even know him!* I cautioned myself.

"Hello, I'm Phil," he said, and so it began. That day we became fast friends, talking well into the night after everyone else had gone to sleep. The next morning I had to get home, but we arranged for Phil to come into town with Celine to see me a few days later. From the second he arrived at my house, we picked right up from where we'd left off, talking about our families, school, friends, failed relationships, and anything else we could think of. He made fun of my New York accent, and I mimicked his Massachusetts tones. And then, when there was nothing to discuss or tease each other about, he leaned in and kissed me. Time was kind enough to slow down so I could memorize every detail and commit it to memory forever. That kiss was the most sobering experience of my entire young life.

As he got ready to leave, I gave Phil a piece of paper with every possible way to reach me on it. Perhaps a bit of my inner wild child remained in that I wanted to challenge the fates, but I told him, "I'm not going to take any of your numbers. The next move is yours to make."

He didn't call for a couple days, but as soon as he did, our relationship was marked by horrendous, but joyful, long-distance bills. Two weeks of nightly marathon phone sessions gave me the strength to take the plunge and make a trip to Massachusetts. Inside, I was a bundle of nerves because I was worried that I was falling so hard that if it didn't work, I'd land in a pile of tissues. Terrified, I admitted my fears to my friends, and they handed out age-old platitudes: "Don't get your hopes up," one said. "Long distance doesn't work," another warned. "Just have fun—you're too young to get serious," added a third.

It was true that at age 19 I didn't need to be bothered by a long-distance relationship—or any significant union for that matter. Juggling those sentiments back and forth in my mind during my ride to see Phil, I decided that he wasn't really my boyfriend, but he wasn't just a friend either. *Well, then, what is he?* I fretted.

He answered that question when he kissed me at his front door. That day I learned that it only takes a second to settle questions concerning destiny—and I knew I was destined to be in his arms at that very second.

Later, I met all of Phil's friends, and the evening ended with him taking me for a walk so we could have the alone time I'd been dreaming about for weeks. "I think we should pursue this thing and take it day by day," he said. It wasn't easy, but it wasn't so hard either. Sure, there were a few bumps in our long-distance road, but we fell in love quickly over the telephone. In many respects, we were lucky, because if our relationship had progressed under normal circumstances, we probably wouldn't have learned so much about each other. On the phone we didn't have tender lips and sweet touches—we just had our words.

For a year and a half, we had the luxury of romancing each other with the feelings we were forced to verbalize each night. Time passed, and I received my associate's degree from The Rock. And the only thing I could do was transfer to a college in Boston to be near Phil. After graduation, I moved in with him and his mom and dad—it was a time of adjustment, including being part of a large family, which is new territory for me. Now we're saving for our future. The pennies in our piggy bank grow each day, and the money will go toward our wedding.

Our story is simple but unique, because most people don't allow themselves three years to grow a life. Yet Phil and I didn't just grow as a couple; we also matured as individuals who became more and more confident in ourselves. We think in terms of "us" now—there are no solo discussions anymore because we love each other unconditionally.

As for me, the wild child allowed someone to knock down her walls. She allowed love to make her a better person. Much has changed over these past three years, but one thing hasn't, and I hope it never will: I still get that same feeling when Phil kisses me. It's a feeling that makes me think my stomach has dropped to my feet while my head has become so light it will float away. One kiss and I'm that wild girl again, in the best possible sense of being able to let go and be free.

— Inspired by Suzy from Boston, Massachusetts

Chapter 31

And Now, um, a Word from, uh, Fox Mulder

(Featuring David Duchovny)

David Duchovny, on the day he proposed to Téa Leoni: "I sat Téa down and said, 'I have to ask you something. I have to ask you and I, um, you, um, don't have to, um, answer . . . well, not right now. But possibly—and you might want to think about this, but not right now—but perhaps you could think about marrying me, but I don't really need a response, and this could happen in the future if you really want it to happen, but it's up to you. Just think about it.'

"She just welled up with tears and said one word: 'Yes!'"

Chapter 32

The Mary-a-Thon

"You must enter the race to win."

That was the line that kept playing in my head when I decided to propose to my beloved Mary. For months I'd been racking my brain for a way to pop the question that was completely unique, yet stayed true to Mary's Chinese heritage. That's when I began to think of life as a marathon: First, you decide to sign up for it. Next, through stamina, sheer will, and smarts—not to mention a few deep breaths along the way—you run the race. And at the end of the finish line is a valuable prize. In this case, the win was my life with Mary.

Let's begin at the starting line. This race took place right before Valentine's Day 1994, during a typically frigid Ohio winter. That's when 20 of our closet friends agreed to participate in an event I dubbed "The Mary-a-Thon."

"Honey, *what* are we doing today?" a befuddled Mary asked me when I took her for a walk near frozen Lake Erie on the snow-covered wooden planks that served as a bridge near the water.

"Today we're going to do something new. You're going to pit yourself against our friends in a variety of cool ways. Each time you successfully complete an event, you'll win a secret puzzle piece," I explained.

"This is extremely crazy," she muttered, but went along for the ride. In other words, she entered the race.

The first event brought Mary to a nearby mall. Her job was to ask people who were planted there beforehand for clues. There was a time limit, and my soon-to-be-fiancée had to race around the stores, quiz people, and then find a hidden puzzle piece in a stuffed-animal shop. Then she had to battle with another friend at a virtual-reality-game emporium. Her win meant another puzzle piece.

But Mary wasn't done there. She had to shoot hoops, play darts, race virtual motorcycles, and even stuff her face in a pizza-eating contest. Gooey cheese was dripping off her lips when hostile commandos wearing sunglasses, trench coats, and berets suddenly surrounded her on all sides. "Are you Mary?" one of them demanded.

"Uh, yeah. You know me!" she said, laughing.

"Miss, come with us," said another friend who tried to be very serious as he led Mary to the getaway car. Brandishing their lethal water guns and speaking to her in thick European accents, they blindfolded this game girl and took her on a drive to parts unknown.

"No talking, miss," said one of the six commandos.

"Get over yourselves," Mary shot back. "Oh, and by the way, where are you taking me?"

These thugs were no match for a tough-talking Mary, although they tried to keep up the macho act. "Quiet!" one said, murmuring the directions to the driver. "No, turn left here," he said under his breath. "We can't get lost—he'll kill us!"

Actually, the commandos were my buddies, and their assignment was to stall for time so that I could set up the next part of the day. The only problem was that they *really* got into their roles—45 minutes later, I was agonizing and wondering what had happened to them. Just when I was about to go insane with worry, Mary was led to a beautiful snow-covered public park, where I was anxiously waiting in a horse-drawn carriage.

Gingerly, I pulled her blindfold down, and she smiled when she saw me. "Honey, where are we?" she asked.

"We're almost at the finish line for our event, but the starting point of our lives," I said. She just smiled as I signaled the driver and told him to "take us somewhere special."

After a scenic carriage ride, we left our driver and horse behind a quiet peninsula off of Lake Erie. Grabbing my wonderful girlfriend's gloved hand, I led her to a wooden park bench. "Could you please hand me your puzzle pieces?" I asked. She did so, and we worked at putting the pieces together while breathing in the cold winter air.

Heart sinking, I realized that one of the pieces was missing. Somehow we'd lost the YOU, so our puzzle read: WILL MARRY ME, MARY? It wasn't perfect, but I wasn't disappointed because, like life itself, all races have obstacles and hurdles to get around.

Despite the missing word, Mary was still speechless, so there was only one thing left to do. Dropping to one knee, I pulled out my 50-karat lollipop ring and inquired, "Will YOU marry me?"

"Yes! Yes!" she cried, knowing why I had to use the candy ring. You see, Chinese tradition requires that the real ring be presented at a formal engagement party with both families present, so the lollipop ring would have to do for now.

Later that night, we joined all our friends, including "the commandos." It was a night of food and warm fellowship, which is what usually happens after a tough event. And as for us, Mary passed the "Mary-a-Thon," but I knew that *I* was the one who'd actually won the best prize of all.

— **Inspired by Jason from Cleveland, Ohio**

69. Elation and sheer romance are a potent mix.

70. Lovers never tire of listening to the sound of music.

Chapter 33

The Sounds of Marriage
(Featuring Julie Andrews)

Julie Andrews filled our hearts with the sound of music, but her own was quite empty after a painful divorce. Yet when she met producer-director Blake Edwards more than 35 years ago, she knew that they shared a strong bond. But even a woman with a four-octave range and perfect pitch wasn't humming "Here Comes the Bride" until one fateful night on the telephone.

"I was in the south of France making a movie called *Star!,* and Blake was busy in California working on another film," Julie explains. "He called me one night and said, 'Julie, I'm very excited. Michel Legrand just wrote the most beautiful piece for my movie. Would you listen?'" she recalls.

Just then, Blake pushed a button and the achingly beautiful strains of the piano filled the air. "He played the most gorgeous music over those phone lines," she says. "I was lost in this song, and then suddenly Blake came back on the phone. I said, 'Oh my God. That's lovely.' He said, 'Now, will you marry me?'"

Their union has been going strong for more than three decades—and she says the secret is that they take it one day at a time. "You take it moment by moment because marriage is a hard thing to do," she says. "It's just that simple. Don't look to the future—just make today work." That's what keeps a union grounded in the reality of love instead of the fairy tale. "Instead of having a fantasy of the future and that it will be all bright and beautiful, we just make *today* bright and beautiful. That's within our reach," Julie muses.

"For us, dealing with now makes it work. Of course, it's also nice that we both want it to work. It always takes two," says the screen legend.

Chapter 34

The Chance Encounter

I'm a Long Island girl who was born and raised "old school" Italian. So imagine my shock when my parents came home one day and announced that we were moving to boring, alligator-infested, rural Florida. "My life is over," I told my friends. "Good-bye, city life!"

We packed up, purchased gallons of bug spray, and moved, but I never felt at home. High school was rough because the native Floridians took one look at my father's big car and thought he was a "made man." That infuriated me, but not as much as when the other kids made fun of my Noo Yawk accent. *They* had the language problem if you ask me, because I ordered a "Coke" or a "soda" at a restaurant—every time I heard the word *pop,* I looked around for that person's father.

Sure, I made a few friends, but for the most part I stayed close to my two older sisters because they understood that my heart was back in New York. By the way, the Sunshine State boys never made sense to me. So, not being used to the Southern-gentleman type (I'm not a ma'am!), I was hoping that someone from the neighborhood would invite me out for a slice of pizza. But there *was* no neighborhood, and the pizza was mushy and undercooked.

As if in answer to my prayers, my parents decided that it was time to move again, this time to the bigger city of Miami. Now we were talking—it was like someone had decided to take some of the cool parts of New York and transplant them to a tropical paradise! By this time, I'd graduated from high school and watched my sisters get married. Deep down, I was thrilled for them, but as I tucked each bridesmaid's dress away, I was more certain than ever that I'd never meet the right guy.

What followed were some typical life events: finding an apartment, going to college, and working as a waitress while I tried to land a few modeling gigs. There were a few men who offered to "take care of" me—but it was easy to reject each one of them because there was no real love there.

"I can't believe what my life has become," I told my friends. "I just feel empty." One day I was really feeling that way while driving with my mother around town. Glancing at the traffic to my right, I spotted an angel of a man in the car beside us. "Look, Ma," I said. "How cute is that guy next to us?"

She just shook her head and scolded, "Angie, you don't even know that man! You shouldn't be talking about him!" (Did I mention that Ma was "old school," too?)

In the following weeks, I spotted that "angel man" driving around our neighborhood, and I started to wonder where he lived. My fantasy life began to kick in, and I mused that he was single, very lonely, and driving around just looking for the right woman . . . who was obviously a girl transplanted from New York against her will. Anyone that cute, I reasoned, must also be very bright, sweet, and good-hearted. In my mind, I also decided that he loved ziti, *The Sopranos,* and the sound of a girl with a less-than-faint trace of the Bronx in her voice. *Angie, wake up!* I told myself. *You've really lost it now.*

One evening my gaze was drawn to the front door of the restaurant I worked in. Wouldn't you just know it—that angelic guy I'd seen around was actually walking toward the hostess station. He was tall, *and* he appeared to be Italian! I wanted to drop to my knees and weep, but instead I grabbed a menu and made a beeline for his table.

"Hello, I'm Angie, and I'll be your waitress," I managed once he was seated. Steadying my hand, I could barely take his order.

He also seemed a little taken aback. "Do I know you from somewhere?" he asked while his warm brown eyes examined my face quizzically.

"Um, maybe you've seen me around town," I lied, smiling inside. I couldn't believe that just maybe he'd noticed me in my car that day. Yeah, right. And my fairy godmother was about to walk out of the kitchen with size-eight glass slippers that read "Manolo Blahnik" on the bottom.

"I'm Jimmy," he said with a grin. Two hours later, my new friend decided to leave more than a tip: He asked me out on a date, which just about stopped my heart. But the sad fact is that I had to decline because I was dating someone else, and we'd promised each other that it was exclusive. A woman of my word, I watched my fantasy man leave the restaurant looking a tad bummed out.

As soon as I got home, I decided to mainline my drug of choice: I dove spoon-first into the fudge ripple and decided that my life truly was in the pits now. But Jimmy and I kept bumping into each other through what turns out were mutual friends. These same pals began to tell each of us that we were alike, and I had to think that maybe we *did* have something in common besides the uncanny way we liked to frequent the same spots.

Eventually I broke up with my boyfriend and decided that I was ready to date Jimmy—but now it was his turn to decline my invitation, because our so-called friends had told him that I was a very serious type of girl who was interested in marriage, and he wasn't sure if he was ready for that yet.

Five years passed, and I grew up and expanded my social circle. Everyone was thrilled when I started dating a plastic surgeon, except for me. Dying to break up with him, I waited until he passed his boards because I didn't want to cause him any undue stress. Soon enough, it was time to say good-bye to him. That same night, I decided to celebrate my new solo life with a friend.

Across the restaurant, my eyes were drawn to the same angel face I'd seen driving in the car next to me with my mother that day so many years before. Jimmy and I locked eyes, and that was it—we haven't left each other's side in three years. We're engaged, and we marvel about how chance, or something else, brought us together.

Consider the following: Jimmy moved to Miami the same time I did, also swearing that he'd never meet anyone because he didn't feel at home outside of New York. He was always sure that once he settled down he'd move back to the Big Apple. He also confessed that, when we first met, he figured he'd be single for life, yet he knew that I'd rock that plan. So by the time we ran into each other again, he was doomed in the best possible sense of the word.

Jimmy knew that his single days were out of his system, and that our true home was in the state of Florida. It's our home because of each other. But that doesn't mean we can't share a mean baked ziti under a palm tree.

— Inspired by Angie from Miami, Florida

Chapter 35

Where There's a Will
(Featuring Will Smith and Jada Pinkett-Smith)

Where there's a will, there's a way to make your marriage work. In other words, Will Smith and his lovely missus, Jada Pinkett-Smith, have a beautiful marriage. Here, they reveal how they do it:

Will: "I'm blessed, and it's because Jada has taught me the secret of a successful relationship. It's just hard, cold, brutal, blatant, unadulterated honesty with one another. There is no such thing in our relationship as a little lie or a big lie. It's only ever the truth, whether it's about a performance in a film or a new dress. It really hurts sometimes, but it's the truth, and we deal with it at that moment and go on with no regrets."

Jada: "We have a wonderful marriage. We really enjoy each other and spend a lot of time enjoying each other. Is it perfect? No. Will has about two days a year when he's in a bad mood. Do I nag him? No. Mama just gets out of his way, figuring that only two days makes me a lucky woman—many women have more than two days. And I also figure that Will's imperfection is what makes him so perfect for me because I'm not perfect either."

Will: "Any woman that you put first—and make your first thought and first action of every day, and last thought and last action of every day—well, she will love you to the moon. I know what my priorities are: I don't let a day go past that she doesn't feel like the queen of the world and definitely the queen of my heart. And what you get from that is you get a lot of freedom to sort of not be there some of the time that you probably should have been there, and time when you can explore your other creative avenues. But I make sure every single day that she knows she's the queen of my world."

LOVE LESSONS

76. While it might be better to give, it's also pretty good to receive.

77. Oh, and the gift of produce produces great results.

Chapter 36

Fifty Birthday Wishes

Ever since I was a little girl, I refused to accept the idea of a birth*day*. For me, birthdays have always been a big deal because you've lived another year. I know that's reward enough, but I just don't think one day is enough to celebrate something so big. You need a birth *month*.

Call me greedy, but I wanted an entire four and a half weeks to be joyful about the accomplishment of surviving another 365 days in this tough world—so you can just imagine how I felt as my 50th birthday crept into my consciousness. With the calendar inching toward my big day in October, I told my amazing boyfriend, Matt, about the "birth month" plan. He'd been there for me for so many years, yet he quickly dismissed my idea. I let it go because I was happy enough to just have him in my life. After all, our romance was one for the books....

Matt and I had known each other since 1974, when I worked for his father's automotive business while going to nursing school in Maine. We quickly developed a warm friendship and confided everything to each other. Eventually, time passed and I left that job and moved to Illinois, but I maintained contact with Matt. Quite happily, I called to congratulate him when he announced his impending wedding.

Soon it was my turn: I met a nice man, married him, and then sadly got divorced. Moving from Illinois to Los Angeles, I kept in touch with Matt, who'd stayed in picture-postcard Maine. There weren't many birthdays that went by where I didn't call Matt and vice versa. When I went to Maine to visit my mother, I always tried to get together with Matt and his father. I finally decided to move closer to my mother and was happily surprised when Matt called me one day and asked me out for dinner. That's when he informed me that he'd split with his wife. *Danger, Will Robinson!* my brain warned. Since I wasn't sure if his separation was temporary or permanent, I decided to stay out of it and just remain friends with him.

Meanwhile, Matt moved out of his house and began to talk divorce. Eventually, we knew that our friendship was something deeper, so we began to date each other. "We're never getting married," I told him. "Since we're too old to have kids, there's no reason to get hitched." He agreed to this; however, when he wanted to move his business to another part of Maine, I was in a serious quandary. "I'm only going if you come along," he told me.

Two houses were sold, his divorce became final, and we finally moved in together. It was a little less than two months before my 50th birthday when the last U-Haul truck pulled away, and although I still clung to the monthlong party plan, I knew that it was impossible to pull off since our lives were so crazed at the moment. There was my stuff, his stuff, and our stuff to unpack—plus tons of work to do on the property and endless little expenses that came up each day. I hoped that on my actual birthday we could take a break and celebrate, but you have to be practical . . . or do you?

Exactly 50 days before my birthday, the UPS man knocked on the door and said, "Lois? I have a package for you."

I wasn't expecting anything, so I quickly opened the accompanying card, which read: "Happy birthday. I love you." I thought that this was strange since my big day was still almost two months away. Yet I loved the box of imported Italian cheeses and, even better, the smile on Matt's face when he returned home from work that day. "I thought there might be something better than your birth month," he explained. "I wanted to do a 50-day countdown to your 50th birthday."

The why was the best gift of all: "I missed so many of these birthdays in person that I need to make up for lost time."

"Oh, honey, you don't have to—and it's so expensive," I said, but he just laughed and got some plates for the cheese. *Is it possible that there's someone even more romantic than I am when it comes to celebrating life's milestones?* I wondered. *Am I really that lucky?* The next morning, another UPS truck pulled up to our house. "I have something for you," said the friendly driver, who handed me two dozen long-stemmed red roses with a card that read: "Happy birthday, from someone who totally adores you."

"You're crazy!" I told Matt, secretly counting down the hours until the next surprise. He didn't disappoint—the next day, the UPS man was back with a chuckle and another sweet card, along with a massive cardboard box. Inside was a gardening kit—you see, months before moving into our new home, I'd told Matt that it was my dream to someday have a backyard where I could start my own vegetable garden. So he'd given me a tomato cage, a bag of organic soil, some fertilizer, and a few tomato plants.

"As much as I love the gift, the real present is that this man was listening to what I was saying," I told my mother later. What followed over the next few weeks were boxes of chocolate, pretty clothes, specially imported olive oil, cards and flowers galore, a Betty Boop music box that crooned "I Want to Be Loved by You," and a beautiful porcelain ring box.

One day I looked around and realized that I'd received about 150 roses by then for my 50-day countdown. I didn't have enough vases, which is just about the happiest dilemma in the whole world. That night I lovingly told Matt, "Honey, you can stop already. I love you, and I know you love me. Thank you *so* much."

"Okay, you're absolutely right. I'll stop," he said in a serious voice.

The next day I received California strawberries hand-dipped in white chocolate. They sat in a beautiful red-velvet heart-shaped box that even impressed my daily caller, the UPS man. "Someone *really* likes you," he mused.

As my actual birthday neared, I told Matt that I didn't want to go out, but would prefer a quiet dinner in. After a lovely evening in our home, I thought we might go for a walk and watch the beautiful Maine sun set for the day. I certainly didn't expect him to give me anything that night except his love and time. So when he dropped to one knee at our new dining-room table, I was shocked. "I have your final gift," he said, producing a beautiful diamond engagement ring from his pocket.

"But we weren't going to get married!" I cried.

"Honey, why do you think I sent you a ring box?" Matt asked with that huge smile I'd loved for years.

In response, the only thing I could say was a simple "Yes." It was the best gift of all, and the one I least expected. As for the 50 gifts, Matt later told me, "I hope this has cured you of your birth-month plan."

"You're right. A birthday month isn't enough," I teased. "Next year, I'll have 51 days before my birthday." But the best thing of all is going to be waking up next to Matt each and every day.

— **Inspired by Lois from Brunswick, Maine**

Chapter 37

The Lovers' Secret Garden

There are times in life when the message of love is
delivered for a small handling fee.

Both men and women adore getting fresh flowers, but there's a big difference between sending a ravishing red rose and a tender tulip. Each bud or sprig speaks volumes—all you have to do is read between the blooms. So here's a handy "petal primer":

- A red rose says "I love you."

- A deep red rose says, "I adore you."

- A white rose says, "My love for you is pure."

- A yellow rose says, "We're good friends" or "I'm jealous."

- A pink rose says, "You're my first love."

- A dark pink rose says, "Thank you very much."

- A peach flower of any kind says, "Please, let's get together."

- A purple flower of any kind says, "I remain true."

- A lavender flower of any kind says, "I fell in love with you the minute I met you."

- A daisy says, "I'm romantic and loyal."

- Sweet peas say, "I'd like to thank you."

- Tulips say, "I love you, and the simplicity of that love is what matters."

- A hyacinth says, "I feel joyous in your presence."

- A sprig of lavender says, "I'm committed to you" or "I messed up."

- Heather says, "I really think you're amazing."

- Mums say, "I hope for our future."

- And finally, that mixed bouquet on sale at the supermarket for $3.99 says, "Honey, I know you love getting flowers. And I love making you happy." (Trust us.)

Part V

Lessons on
Real Love

*"If there ever comes a day when we can't be together,
keep me in your heart. I'll stay there forever."*

— Winnie the Pooh

Chapter 38

American Airlines Flight 866

The six soldiers had been stationed in Iraq for more than a year's time, fighting a war that seemed to have no end. They longed for simple pleasures such as hugging their wives or seeing their newborn children for the first time. They dreamed of hot dogs, baseball, Wal-Mart, and, most of all, the ability to walk down the street without thinking that it might be the last stroll they ever took.

After months of longing, it appeared as if their wishes were about to come true. One day, after eluding roadside terrorist bombers and bloodthirsty hijackers, they returned to their base to find a letter that read: "For your service to your country, you will each be granted two weeks' leave back home."

If they could have sprouted wings, the soldiers would have left that night, but it simply wasn't possible. Instead, Uncle Sam, ever the sport, gave them each a coach seat on American Airlines. The journey would be long—including stops in Germany, London, and Dallas—before they'd even get to board planes to reach their individual homes.

But something funny happened when the soldiers boarded the Dallas flight back in the good old U. S. of A.: All eight passengers in the first-class cabin leapt to their feet when the men appeared, almost as if they were giving the boys in uniform a standing ovation. And that wasn't enough for those who were about to embark on a flight of fine dining and cushy leather seats. The first-class passengers each approached a soldier and insisted that they swap seats.

"You mean you'll sit in coach and let us sit up here?" one amazed soldier asked, not exactly believing that these strangers were being so kind.

When the swap was almost done, the last two first-class passengers were forlorn. They wanted to give up their seats, too, but couldn't find any more soldiers.

"The soldiers were very, very happy, and the whole aircraft had a different feeling," flight attendant Lorrie Gammon told *The Dallas Morning News*. Her flying partner, Candi Spradlin, said that small acts of goodwill like this one change everyone's mood. "If nothing else, those soldiers got a great homecoming," she said.

Chapter 39

Advertising for Love

Love shouldn't cost a thing, but it actually did come with a price tag for me: $752, to be exact. That's what I paid when I decided to propose to Sarah. I'd taken out a quarter-page ad in our local newspaper to ask my true love to marry me. But I never expected an actual story on my romantic gesture to run on the front page of the paper!

The big problem was that I had to hide that front page, complete with our favorite picture above the fold. After all, I didn't want Sarah to see the story before she spotted the ad! So over breakfast, I handed her the middle of the paper, which, thankfully, didn't elicit any strange questions. Flipping around, she got to page 47 and quickly began to cry. When she looked up, I was standing in the middle of the kitchen holding a ring.

It was a lovely moment because we met through friends five years ago and have been inseparable ever since. I'd even felt bad because I couldn't afford the $2,000 it cost to take out a full-page ad in the paper. But none of that mattered when the universe decided to lend us a romantic hand. (By the way, Jim Brickman allowed me to reprint a verse of his song "Love of My Life" in the ad. The love of *my* life was very touched.)

— Inspired by Bob from Flint, Michigan

Chapter 40
Kite Strings
(Featuring Jeff Bridges)

The photograph has seen better days: It's faded, folded, and torn at the corner. And with the care of a man handling a newborn infant, Jeff Bridges carefully takes the keepsake out of his wallet.

"I've been married for [almost 30] years," he says. "At all times, I keep a photograph in my pocket of the very first words I ever uttered to my wife, Susan."

The year was 1975. Beautiful Susan Geston was working as a maid at a Montana dude ranch, while boyishly handsome Jeff Bridges, a 27-year-old young buck at the time, was filming the movie *Rancho Deluxe* there for the summer.

"I walked up to her and asked her for a date, and she said no," he explains. "I was totally coldcocked. I was so crestfallen that the set photographer who was in the vicinity took a snap of both her and me."

Jeff recalls that Susan laid it on the line. "She said, 'Oh, you think you Hollywood guys can come in here and get all the local girls?'" he recalls, smiling. "Incidentally, at the time my future wife said this to me, she had a broken nose and two black eyes from a car accident."

Susan did give him a second glance from behind her bruises and remarked, "Of course, it *is* a small town. Maybe I'll see you around."

The rest is history: The two ran into each other in a local bar a few nights later, danced and kissed, and "that was it for me. I was gone," Jeff says.

Some 15 years ago, he received the photo in the mail from the makeup man on that shoot. Jeff laughs and says, "The note read: 'I thought you might like this picture. It's you asking some beautiful local girl out.'

"And now it's all these years later, and people ask me the secret to a happy marriage. I really do think it's about the communication. Keeping the lines open. And for me, it really was love at first sight. I was really bowled over by Susan right away, and that never stopped.

"Marriage gives you a reason to make a living, which is to support your family," he says. "You also feel grounded because you're not trying to find a mate. You're not running around doing crazy stuff. You've got a home base.

"My wife is home," he concludes. "It's like she's holding the kite string—I can fly around, but I always have somewhere to come back to."

LOVE LESSONS

87. Realize that love can be gone in the blink of an eye.

88. In the worst moments, take a deep breath, keep your seat belt on, and drive the course.

89. In times of trauma, operating on faith is the best way.

Chapter 41

The Accident

The countdown was on: It was the day before Thanksgiving in Philly, and the streets were jammed with frenzied shoppers rushing home with their turkey fixings. I wanted the world to feel sorry for me as I was driving home from work in very heavy traffic. Two streetlights away from my apartment, I was still just inching along. Like every other person on the road, I was brimming with impatience. There was so much to do at home because I was making a big holiday dinner for my boyfriend, Patrick, and our families. Surely I didn't have time to waste just sitting in the car and watching life pass me by.

A few car lengths up the road, I suddenly felt very, very guilty. *Oh my God, we're backed up because of an accident,* I thought. *Here I am thinking that I don't have time to make stuffing, and someone else is getting a call tonight saying that their loved one is seriously hurt or has been killed.* Just ahead of me was a nasty scene filled with police cars, blaring sirens, ambulances, and a tow truck that was lifting the twisted metal of what was once a pickup onto its flatbed. As I quickly glanced over at the mangled mess, a sick feeling crept into the pit of my stomach. *That looks exactly like Patrick's truck,* I realized, as my pulse began to race.

I'd been dating Patrick for more than two years, and we were deeply in love. Now he might be hurt, and I couldn't believe that what had seemed like someone else's heartache could be my own. Making a quick right turn, I parked my car, flew out the door, and ran over to the accident site. "Miss, excuse me—you can't go over there," a police officer said, putting out his arm to prevent me from reaching the scene.

My entire body was shaking, but I stopped walking. My eyes stayed riveted to the pickup that looked like a sculpture of chaos—which I now knew had certainly belonged to my Patrick. The truck was completely smashed into snarled bits, and the front windshield was gone. "Officer!" I cried. "You have to tell me what happened to the driver of that truck!"

"Miss, I just arrived on the scene. I'm not sure," he said, looking at me a little too sympathetically now. "All I know is that they took someone to the hospital two blocks away from here. They rushed him right over."

"Is he . . . is he okay?" I stammered, choking back tears.

"You'd have to ask at the hospital," said the officer. "Please be careful going over there," he added. "You look very upset."

Upset was an understatement: I felt like I was sleepwalking as I made my way back to my car. I couldn't help but think, *Patrick's truck looks like it was smashed by a bulldozer.* Although I wasn't exactly sure how my feet were still working, I ran as fast as I could to the hospital. It was like I was floating through some kind of nightmare.

"There was a car accident!" I sputtered to the emergency-room receptionist, tears flowing down my cheeks. "My boyfriend—his name is Patrick!" I couldn't say much more.

"Let me take you to his room," said the woman behind the desk.

What followed was a sight I'll never forget, and certainly one that redefined every Thanksgiving holiday since: "Hi, baby. You better cook me something really good tomorrow because I have this nasty cut on my finger," Patrick said, smiling as he sat up in bed and waved his injured pinkie.

At that moment, I fell even more deeply in love with Patrick and the universe. It was also the day I truly realized how much this man meant to me. As I tell him now, "I think God put it in perspective for me. When I saw your car, I hit the lowest low—but when I saw that you were okay, it was the highest high. At that moment, I knew that there was nobody else in the world for me but you."

In the days that followed the accident, I told Patrick I loved him about a million times. And I didn't need to grab the wishbone off the turkey when we finally had dinner—there was nothing more to wish for, other than the man sitting across the table from me with a bandage on his pinkie finger.

— Inspired by Lana from Philadelphia, Pennsylvania

LOVE LESSONS

90. If you set something free, it just might show up in your driveway.

91. Patience is a tough virtue.

92. It takes a strong couple to combat aching combined with longing.

Chapter 42

Jonah and Me

There are people who are worth the wait—to that end, I've spent almost my entire life waiting for Jonah.

As a child, I didn't realize that I was biding time until he entered my life. My days were spent living a carefree, all-American life in a small town called Brownsville, Texas. I was a "lifer"—that is, I spent every day of my life in that town.

Jonah, on the other hand, was like a roadrunner in that he'd lived his life in so many places. In 1984, he moved to Brownsville and settled into a house up the street from my own. We rode bikes and went to the park together, and when he announced that his family would be packing up and moving again, I shed a few tears. You see, I had a huge crush . . . on his older brother.

The years passed, and I entered high school. One day I looked up from my pile of books and saw a familiar face: Cruising the hallways was none other than Jonah, but he looked right through me and didn't say a word. *Do I look so different?* I wondered. *Am I ugly now? Or maybe he saw that pimple on my right cheek.* Dejected, I hid behind my locker door and watched him walk away.

Almost as if my crush had been lying dormant, it was suddenly revived—but this time it had nothing to do with his sibling. Jonah was just about the handsomest boy in all of Texas, if you asked me. My friends thought it was crazy: Here I was, a junior, but I had my eye on a lowly sophomore. I'd even stake him out on those hot spring days outside the basketball court where he practiced with the team. Just the hope that Jonah would say a few words to me made it worth the wait. One day he ran up and said, "Hey, I know you! You used to live up the street from me when I was a little kid. I'm Jonah."

"Oh, I think I remember you," I lied, while my teenage heart beat so rapidly that it was like I'd just done ten laps on that court. In the love department, this conversation was nothing if not a slam dunk.

Summer arrived, and one day when my parents told me to go outside and "find something to do," I wallowed in the boredom of my room. "Honey, you have a phone call," my dad eventually yelled to me.

"Hiya," I said, thinking it was one of my equally bored girlfriends.

"Hi, it's Jonah," said the male voice on the other end. "I was wondering if maybe you'd like to go to a movie."

"You can't go," my father said moments later, after I'd begged to go. "You and Mom are leaving tomorrow to visit Grandma in Knoxville. You need to help your mother pack."

I would have jumped off the building, but our home was only two stories tall. My entire world collapsed, and I didn't pack with a good attitude. Smooshing the clothes into the suitcase, I glared at my mother. The idea of turning down a date with my crush was certainly equal to being sentenced to life in prison—or at least two extra semesters of geometry.

My misery didn't end there, though. When I returned from Knoxville, I called Jonah to see if we could have a rain check on that date. "I wish I could go, but I'm packing," he said.

My entire system went into red alert, but I remained hopeful when I asked, "For a vacation? Are you taking a summer trip?"

"Nah," he said, casually. "While you were gone, my dad decided that we're moving to McAllen."

Clearly, my life was over. My only reprieve was when Jonah got very quiet and then blurted out, "Do you think I could call you from time to time?" Of course I said yes.

Even though my girlfriends said he'd never call me, sure enough, he did. And somehow the fact that McAllen was about an hour away made our budding relationship even more exciting. But then, as the months passed, the relationship began to fizzle. Teenagers have too much on their minds, and any kind of distance can often be just too much trouble.

I went on with my life, and Jonah lived his own, but I never forgot him. In fact, days after he graduated from high school, I ran into him. "Maybe you remember me—we used to know each other as kids," I needled him.

Jonah hugged me and agreed to come to a house party I was having. To say that it was a love reunion wouldn't be exactly accurate. Arriving with a couple of his buddies, Jonah only stayed for an hour. But how could I be upset with him? He had a lot on his mind, especially since he was shipping out for boot camp in just a few days. Figuring that I wouldn't see him again for a long time, I said a silent prayer that he'd be safe.

The next day I was sitting in a chair by my bedroom window when I heard a car door slam. Seconds later, Jonah was pounding on my front door. "Let's spend the day together," he said with a big smile, which I returned tenfold. One day turned into two, and then I had to drive him to his uncle's house and say good-bye. Kissing in the moonlight, I blinked back tears and said, "Please at least write to me. Let me know that you're—"

"I'll be fine," he broke in, kissing me harder. "Now don't you go getting another crush on my brother," he said with a smile. "I'm the one for you."

During the next few months, Jonah did write to me, and I answered every letter. On the day he flew home from basic training, I was standing at the front gate of the military base with my entire body on high alert. A blissful week of togetherness followed before he had to leave for Hawaii for advanced training.

"I'll be fine," he repeated the night before he left me alone again in that small Texas town.

It turns out that *I* wasn't fine, though. After four months of Jonah being so far away, I broke up with him, blaming it on the frustration of the distance. I tried to put on a happy face—I even tried dating other guys, but it just wasn't the same.

Then one day I picked up the phone to call Jonah. Finding out that the last number I had for him had been disconnected, I wrote him a letter. Weeks passed, but Jonah finally did call. He was now living in Washington, D.C., but we decided that it was time we really gave this relationship a chance. I soon joined him . . . and we've been together ever since. We even got to spend two beautiful, romantic weeks in Hawaii.

A few months later, Jonah requested leave from the military and came back to Texas because his mother was in the hospital. "Life is fragile," he told me. "And we've wasted so much time. . . ." Not long after this, he asked me to marry him. Three days later, we decided to skip the formalities and go ahead and tie the knot in front of a justice of the peace.

Our lives together began with his being stationed in the lush tropical playground of Hawaii, but we soon came back to the mainland. Yet there was one additional move that I couldn't participate in: Jonah was deployed to Kuwait, and I found myself back where it all started in Brownsville. It was there that I heard the news that my husband was being sent even farther away to Korea.

"Most military families have to spend a lot of time apart," Jonah told me one night when we were back in each other's arms. "We're lucky because we have phone calls, cards, and letters—we get to talk to each other, and some couples aren't so lucky."

Recently, Jonah was shipped off to the war in Iraq. The night before he left, we couldn't sleep and just held each other until the faint morning sun came to remind us that tomorrow never forgets to show up, especially when you least want to see it.

That day, we drove to a local gym, where I waited for my husband to walk away from me and join the rest of the men and women who would soon be fighting for our country—and their own lives. All those families . . . all those tears. . . . Jonah tried to keep it lighthearted because he was trying very hard not to cry, too. A few minutes before he had to walk into that gym and maybe never come back, I hugged him and kissed him hard, although I could barely see his face through my blurry tears. I just knew that this was the last time I'd ever see my precious Jonah.

"I love you. I will always love you," I told him, hugging him once more and wanting it to last forever.

What do you do when your life is up for grabs? You go home, eat breakfast, and then go to work. You cry all day long, especially when you run into the other wives in town whose lives are just like yours. Jonah is a war hero, and he calls me almost every day. I've gotten quite spoiled by the fact that I haven't had to go more than 48 hours without hearing his beautiful voice. When I pass 24 hours, I get very nervous. But I console myself with the knowledge that this country has been kept safe by military families for generations. They've done their time, and now it's my turn to do mine.

Jonah and I have been married for eight years, and this will be our first Christmas apart. I'm dealing with it one day at a time. It's devastating, but my husband is alive, and I'm not pessimistic anymore. We have Christmas for the rest of our lives to spend together. But now, I wait. . . .

Epilogue: Jonah is home on leave right now for two weeks. Hitting the answering machine, he heard the news that our story would be in a book. "What book?" he says, calling me over with a big smile on his face. "What did you tell them?"

"Oh, I can't quite remember," I lie. "But it has lots to do with our love."

"That isn't a book—it's 100 books," he teases back.

— **Inspired by Patricia from Brownsville, Texas**

LOVE LESSONS

93. Love can survive the ride of life.

94. Blissfulness is not just remembering to remember, but writing it down, too.

Chapter 43

The Letter

There's no big story here. This is just about a letter that I once wrote to my husband, which explains what our being together means to me.

Frank and I met when I was 15 and he was 18, and no one figured that we'd ever make it, but we did. We're still growing in our relationship, which is how I figure God intended it. And that's why I wrote him this love note, which I hope you'll be able to appreciate as well.

Hi Sweetie,

I just wanted to thank you for joining me on the ride of a lifetime.

Remember how young and daring we were when we first met? We were willing to take risks and, thus, climbed onto the roller coaster of life. We were filled with excitement, fear, and uncertainty about what lay ahead. Starting out, we chugged along and climbed the first hill. It wasn't too steep, so we were able to take in the newness that was sweet and wild. Reaching the top was thrilling, but when we peered over the side, doubt crept in. We worried, <u>Can we make it? Is this a mistake?</u>

Holding on for dear life, we started to descend. We hit the bumps, twisting and turning, and we were tossed every which way. For three years, we rode like that, feeling the rhythm and the heat—it was like a dance.

Then it came time to decide if we should keep riding the coaster or get off. To keep going we needed more riders, so our sons were born. This is when the ride got crazy, because we had no manual. There was a lot of trial and error, and so many cuts and bruises—both little and big. We were always trying to mend so that we could keep going. And we kept holding on. . . .

There were times when the ride slowed down, and we were able to relax. Then, without warning, the momentum would pick up, pitching us into tunnels of darkness. These contained doors of illness, death, lost jobs, and loss of self. We almost let go, but that's when we saw the faint light—and we reached out for it, gaining hope and gathering strength.

Whenever the roller coaster of life needed fixing, we'd call up the only repairman there is, and He'd see the problem and make His adjustments as only He can. Now, after 30-plus years of marriage, we're still taking the ride. Still unsure of what lies ahead, we're moving slower, but easier, and the ride is stronger and sweeter. Near the end, the roller coaster will be replaced by rocking chairs, but we'll still hold on, loving each other and savoring the sweetness of our lives. The ride of life will continue on with our sons and grandkids.

I just wanted to say thank you for sharing the ride of life. The risk was worth it, and I look forward to our next thrill.

I love you,

Me

— Inspired by Adele from Charleston, South Carolina

LOVE LESSON

95. Magnetism means a lot, but you still need a good pair of shoes to walk the walk of love. . . .

Chapter 44

Walk the Walk
(Featuring Lauren Bacall)

Lauren Bacall and Humphrey Bogart: It was written in the stars, but their romance was played out on the asphalt.

Ask her what the most romantic thing Bogie ever did for her was, and Lauren says, "One night Humphrey Bogart called me at two in the morning and said, 'I'm in Malibu, and you're in Los Angeles. I don't have a car, but I'm coming to meet you. I'm just going to start walking down the highway, and you'll see me in about ten hours.'

"I knew he wanted me to pick him up, but I said, 'I love you—start walking,'" Lauren recalls.

Yes, it was tough love from a tough broad. But there was a little compassion on her part, and a surprise, too. "Of course, I did feel sorry for him, so I got in my car," says the screen legend. "Driving down Highway 101, I saw this figure in the darkness with a smile on his face and a white daisy in his lapel.

"Sure enough, it was Bogie."

© Big Picture News Inc.

Chapter 45

The Terminal

To refresh your memory, here is Sam and Jessica's story, which we began in the Introduction.

They met at dusk, which is probably the only time something beautiful could happen at an airport. All it took was a man, a woman, and space—the scary part was bridging the gap. In this case, it was a distance of about 20 feet, and she refused to perform the old shy, glance-past-each-other dance. Instead, she looked directly at him, and what followed could only be described as magic.

She was the bolder of the two, which explains why a rational woman 33 years of age would invade a total stranger's personal space. (Of course, the 38-year-old man's broad shoulders; dark, curly hair; and warm eyes were also greatly to blame.) Maybe his eyes gave her silent permission to keep walking toward him until only inches separated their faces. That's when she took a deep breath and gave him a hug.

"Hello, I'm home," Jessica announced with all the bravado she could muster. Inside, she was thinking, *This is absolutely insane, but it's the only thing I can say to this man because he looks like home to me.* Win or lose, she had to say those exact words because they were true—and sometimes the truth is all you have.

Life is a series of tiny moments. Sam could have jolted back in shock, walked past Jessica, or even called for airport security. But he didn't. Instead, he felt an immediate connection. "It's good to have you home," he said, not skipping a beat. He didn't quite know where those words came from—he simply knew that he had to say them because his entire being felt them.

What started as an unlikely greeting between strangers in a strange land moved on to the stages of modern courtship, including e-mails and late-night phone calls that lasted until dawn. It wasn't long before Sam and Jessica knew that life would be unbearable unless they could be together. So she packed her bags and moved from Boston to Chicago to live with the soul mate she'd searched for all her life. People who met them, even the ones who didn't believe in love at first sight, couldn't deny it: These two were living the dream.

A life was built on love, respect, and trust. Jessica and Sam's union wasn't forged easily because it came with all the baggage of the past: Her scars were inside *and* out because she'd endured domestic violence, and the only time she'd ever heard the words "I love you" in the past were as a prelude to another false apology.

As for Sam, he felt that his life had run out of chances. He confessed to Jessica that he'd lost all hope in the possibility of finding love because of a mistake in the past that had left him HIV positive. Sam coped by shielding his heart from everyone . . . until the day that lovely lady told him that he was her home. She gave him back his hope and, in return, he simply presented her with his bruised heart.

Hope and heart are a powerful combination, and this union often touched others. With Sam's gentle guidance and support,

Jessica reunited with sons she hadn't seen in many years. They even visited her two boys in California, blissfully unaware that a happy vacation could turn on a dime. A week after they came home, Jessica developed a nasty cough that she decided was just a vicious cold that was going around. Yet before she knew it, she was admitted into the hospital and diagnosed with pneumonia.

Each day her lungs weakened to the point that the only possibility of saving her life was to place her on a respirator. Her new home was the ICU, and she couldn't talk to her beloved Sam because she was sedated. A week into her stay, doctors presented Sam with devastating news: "We're seeing signs of multiple organ failure," they said.

A strong man who was dealing with his own health fears, Sam nevertheless remained steadfast as he sat by Jessica's side. During the few hours that he slept each night, a loving nurse named Kathy cared for his wife. She also often visited Jessica and Sam during the day and was privy to their beautiful and unusual love story. Kathy knew that in life-or-death situations, strange little things can make all the difference, so one night she walked into Jessica's room with a small boom box and a tape filled with beautiful piano music. Played low by the bedside, the music was a constant companion on those lonely evenings when the hospital was eerily silent, except for the brain-numbing beeps of the life-support machines.

Days turned into more nights, and Jessica remained totally unresponsive due to the sedation required for the life support. A routine set in: Sam took the day shift, and Kathy was "on" for the nights. During one of his vigils, doctors came in to tell Sam that it was hopeless, and he needed to think about taking his wife off the respirator—after which, she was only expected to live a few hours.

"I'll give you my decision tomorrow," Sam said, blinded by his tears as he stroked the limp hand of the woman he loved so much. Then he opened his heart and reminded himself, "Love is giving all you can give and wanting nothing in return, yet getting the world." Now his world was slipping away.

Around midnight that night, a devastated Kathy sat in the room knowing that it could be her last time at Jessica's side. Perhaps that's why she approached her unresponsive patient and got as close to her face as Jessica once did to Sam in the airport. This time it was the nurse who decided to ask a crazy question. She knew she had to say these words because her entire being felt them. "Can you hear the music?" Kathy asked.

A second passed, and then another. Nothing.

And then Jessica squeezed Kathy's hand tightly.

"Okay, then are you enjoying the music that's been playing? People in this hospital think it's just silly," the nurse posed, half-laughing and half-crying at the same time.

Amazingly, Jessica clenched her nurse's hand even tighter, as if to say, "Don't you dare turn off that tape. And leave my machines alone, too."

Over the following weeks, Jessica was taken off the respirator and began to breathe on her own again. Her organs even showed vast signs of improvement. Hope filled the room, but that wasn't the only thing in the vicinity: Several nurses and orderlies, and even a few doctors, began to hang out in the room with the beautiful music and the grateful Jessica and Sam, who were given another chance to live their dream. So what if it wasn't a perfect dream? It was theirs, and that was good enough for them.

The day that Sam wheeled Jess out of the hospital was just about the best day of both their lives.

Months have now passed under the beautiful bliss of normalcy, and the sweetest time is at night, when the two are reunited after a long day.

"Hello, I'm home," Jessica says upon opening the door each evening.

"It's good to have you home," her husband always responds.

— Inspired by Jessica and Sam
from Arlington Heights, Illinois

Afterword

The Faces in the Crowd

We thought we'd end this book on a somewhat lighter note by including a rather unusual fan letter Jim got recently, along with his response.

Dear Jim:

This note isn't to tell you that I felt the icy cold weather in Malaysia because you started to sing or that for the first time in my life romance became tangible when you began to play the piano.

This letter won't tell you that for a short while you managed to carry hundreds of people through a maze of emotions, which is something only the gifted can do.

It's not even to state the fact that 240 people would swear that they saw electricity flow from your fingertips to the piano, like the way chocolate flows through my veins.

Nor will you find me saying that at some point in the evening almost every woman thought about her first love, and every man thought about something exceedingly romantic that they'd probably never admit to their significant other, for fear of seeming too soft and mushy.

You won't find me saying any of those things, because they've been said before.

What this letter <u>will</u> tell you is that the simple things in life happened on that stage while you were playing and singing—and that's the beauty of the human experience. When 200 people gather, it's the little moments that count as inspiration for the masses. Perhaps because of your vantage point on the stage, you didn't see the beauty going on down below. Perhaps you missed:

1. The baby in the third row who cried during the concert, certainly thinking, <u>Bring on the purple dinosaur already.</u>

2. The three old ladies behind me who were reminiscing about "the good old days," while you played a tune they'd never actually heard during any of their days.

3. The girl on my right who was on a first date and was afraid to clap too loudly, as if joy was embarrassing.

4. The guy next to her who tried to put his arm around her chair. It happened very slowly three different times before he accepted a defeat of his own making. It was almost as if early love was embarrassing, too.

5. The two fathers who were pacing back and forth with their babies in their massive arms, trying to keep them quiet so that they wouldn't have to admit that leaving the concert—even for a few minutes—wasn't a happy option for them. Oh, they also claimed loudly that they only loved rock 'n' roll. Uh-huh.

6. The five teenagers who were writing the title of every song you played on their arms just because they're teenagers and needed to do something.

7. The six-year-old girl who dropped her pencil while clapping because you started to sing what she considered to be the most moving song in the

history of her life. Of course, it was "The Rainbow Connection" from _The Muppet Movie._

8. The little two-year-old with the adorable cap and pink jumper who fell asleep despite her best efforts to keep her eyes open during "The Rainbow Connection." Some fans love Jagger and Bowie—she loves Kermit.

9. The security guards who were discussing where to have dinner that night.

10. The boy in the wheelchair who was hoping nobody saw him when he dropped his hamburger under his seat and had to skip the idea of dinner that night.

11. The hundreds of people who kept looking back while they walked out of the arena to try to imprint what had just happened on their brains.

12. And finally, there was the girl who fell in love for the first time with the simple things in life, like your music.

Love,
A Fan

Dear Fan:
Thank you from the bottom of my heart. What you saw that evening was a man onstage, behind a piano, playing for his audience. What you didn't see was the love and appreciation I feel in my own heart for the people who came to listen.
Love,
Jim

Do you have an amazing story about how your love survived the odds? Drop us a love note at **www.jimbrickman.com** or **bigpixnews@aol.com**.

About the Authors

Jim Brickman is one of America's hottest new pop stars. His Grammy-nominated dazzling piano artistry and clever songwriting skills have led to sales of more than six million albums, gold- and platinum-selling recordings, hit PBS concert specials, a weekly syndicated radio show *(Your Weekend with Jim Brickman)*, and four chart-topping songs.

Hits such as "Valentine" and "The Gift" have helped build his reputation as America's most romantic songwriter. In theaters across the country, Jim turns a simple concert stage into an intimate space where imagination takes off, using musical notes to weave a tapestry of emotion, color, and spirit. He is the author of *Simple Things* (with Cindy Pearlman).

For more information about Jim, his VIP Club, and exclusive special offers, please visit: **www.jimbrickman. com**.

Cindy Pearlman is a nationally syndicated writer for the *New York Times Syndicate* and the *Chicago Sun-Times.* Her work has appeared in *Entertainment Weekly, Premiere, People, Ladies' Home Journal, McCall's, Seventeen, Movieline,* and *Cinescape.* Over the past 15 years, she has interviewed Hollywood's biggest stars, who appear in her column "The Big Picture."

Cindy is the co-author of *Simple Things* (with Jim Brickman), *It's Not about the Horse* (with Wyatt Webb), *Born Knowing* (with John Holland), *Flex Ability* (with Flex Wheeler), *I'm Still Hungry* and *To Serve with Love* (with Carnie Wilson), and *Everything about Me Is Fake . . . and I'm Perfect* (with Janice Dickinson).

E-mail: **bigpixnews@aol.com**

love notes

love notes

love notes

love notes

love notes

love notes

love notes

We hope you enjoyed this Hay House book. If you'd like to receive a free catalog featuring additional Hay House books and products, or if you'd like information about the Hay Foundation, please contact:

Hay House, Inc., P.O. Box 5100, Carlsbad, CA 92018-5100

(760) 431-7695 or **(800) 654-5126**
(760) 431-6948 (fax) or **(800) 650-5115 (fax)**
www.hayhouse.com

Published and distributed in Australia by:
Hay House Australia Pty. Ltd. · 18/36 Ralph St. · Alexandria NSW 2015
Phone: 612-9669-4299 · *Fax:* 612-9669-4144 · www.hayhouse.com.au

Published and distributed in the United Kingdom by:
Hay House UK, Ltd. · Unit 62, Canalot Studios · 222 Kensal Rd., London W10 5BN
Phone: 44-20-8962-1230 · *Fax:* 44-20-8962-1239 · www.hayhouse.co.uk

Published and distributed in the Republic of South Africa by:
Hay House SA (Pty), Ltd., P.O. Box 990, Witkoppen 2068
Phone/Fax: 2711-7012233 · orders@psdprom.co.za

Distributed in Canada by:
Raincoast · 9050 Shaughnessy St., Vancouver, B.C. V6P 6E5
Phone: (604) 323-7100 · *Fax:* (604) 323-2600

Sign up via the Hay House USA Website to receive the Hay House online newsletter and stay informed about what's going on with your favorite authors. You'll receive bimonthly announcements about: Discounts and Offers, Special Events, Product Highlights, Free Excerpts, Giveaways, and more!
www.hayhouse.com